INVITATION TO A VOYAGE

Invitation to a Voyage

French-language Poetry of the
Indian Ocean African Islands

Edited by Stephen Gray
Language consultant: Carole Beckett

Protea Book House
Pretoria
2008

The publication of this book was made possible through a generous contribution from the French Institute of South Africa.

Institut Français
d'Afrique du Sud

Liberté • Égalité • Fraternité
RÉPUBLIQUE FRANÇAISE
AMBASSADE DE FRANCE
EN AFRIQUE DU SUD
THE EMBASSY OF FRANCE
IN SOUTH AFRICA

french information centre
centre d'information sur la france contemporaine

Copyright rests with the original of each item and with its translator

© 2008 Stephen Gray for editorial matter, selection and other translations

First editon, first impression in 2008 by Protea Book House

Protea Book House
PO Box 35110, Menlo Park, 0102
1067 Burnett Street, Hatfield, Pretoria
8 Minni Street, Clydesdale, Pretoria
protea@intekom.co.za
www.proteaboekhuis.co.za

Cover design: Hanli Deysel
Map: Magda Geringer
Set in Zapf Calligraphic 801 BT, 10 on 14 pt by Mckore Graphics
Printed and bound by Paarl Print, 22 Oosterland Street, Paarl

ISBN 978-1-86919-169-6

No part of this book may be reproduced or transmitted in any form or by any electronic or mechanical means, including photocopying and recording, or by any other information storage or retrieval system, without written permission from the publisher.

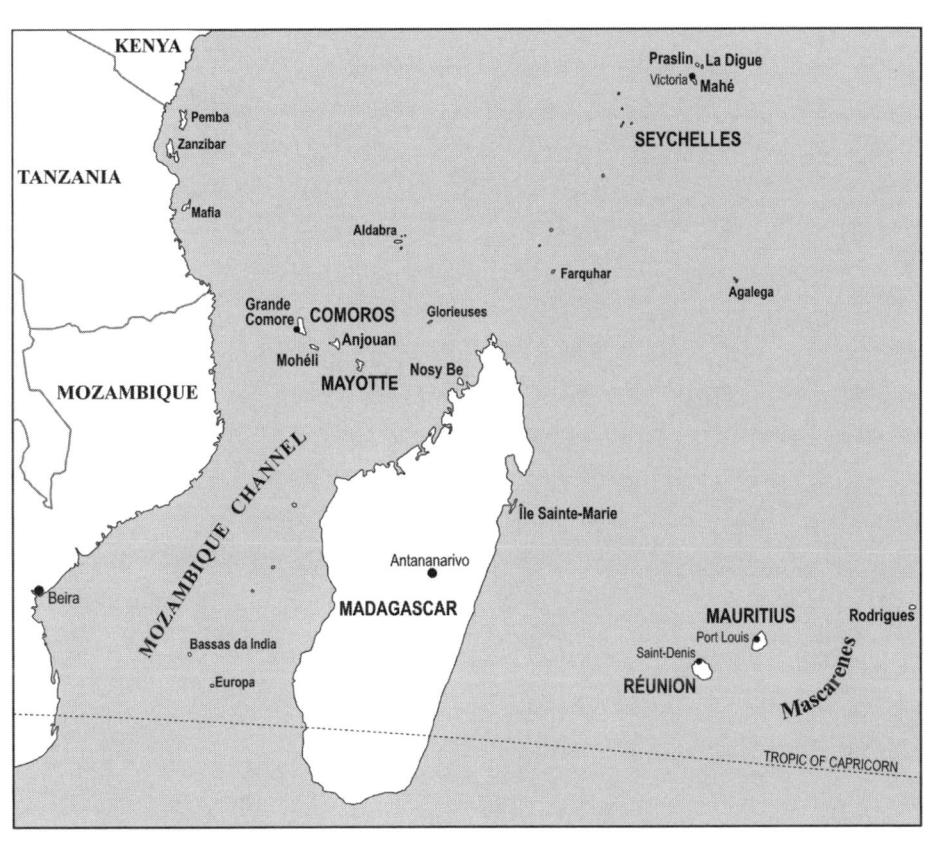

CONTENTS

Introduction	xiii
Notes on Translators	xxxvii
Jacques-Henri Bernardin de Saint-Pierre	1
Reflections on Slavery	2
Alexandre Dumas	4
A Free Man's Song	4
Charles Baudelaire	6
Invitation to a Voyage	6
Exotic Perfume	8
Man and the Sea	8
To a Creole	9
Aan 'n Kreoolse Dame	10
The Albatross	10
Die Albatros	11
Raymond Radiguet	12
Paul and Virginia	12
Assane Y. Diallo	13
Island Words	13
RÉUNION	
Évariste Parny	17
First Song	17
Second Song	18
Fifth Song	18
Sixth Song	19
Ninth Song	20
Eugène Dayot	21
To Colas	21
I the Leper	22
Thanksgiving	22

Charles René Marie Leconte de Lisle	**25**
The Palanquin	25
The Palm-tree	27
Malay Pantoum	28
Song of the Negro Fisherman	30
Stray Dogs	33
Pierre-Claude Georges-François	**35**
Atlas	35
At Saint Marie	36
Louis Ozoux	**39**
A Dionysian Evening	39
'n Aand in Saint Denis	40
André Cazamian	**41**
Native Isle	41
Boris Gamaleya	**42**
To Jean-Jacques Rabéarivelo	42
Alain Belair	**44**
Lil' French Paradise	44
Up There in the Bush	45
Die Vrou, die Man	46
Claire Karm	**48**
Last Postcard	48

MAURITIUS

Robert-Edward Hart	**51**
We're Closing	52
Malcolm de Chazal	**54**
Lemuria	54
Pierre Renaud	**56**
Classified Small	56
Here are Words	57
Édouard J. Maunick	**60**
Pro Memoria	61
Parabasis	62
From South Africa on the Teleprinter	63

Clifford Ng Kwet Chan	**64**
Mea Culpa	64
The Dustbins of the Rich	64
Flashback	65
Jean-Georges Prosper	**68**
Golden Bird	68
Insula Mea	69
Henry Koombes	**71**
The Rictus on an Angel's Face	71
Carl de Souza	**73**
Tamarind Bay	73
Khal	**76**
My skin sings	76
And if I've chosen	77
In Memory of Pierre Poivre of Lyons	77
Sedley Richard Assonne	**78**
He was Called Ali	78

MADAGASCAR

Jean-Joseph Rabéarivelo	**83**
Note on the Tribe of Beggars	84
Here She Stands	86
Your Work	87
Filao	88
Flautists	89
Tall Trees	90
Zebu	92
Last Journal	94
Robert-Jules Allain	**96**
Song of the South	96
Jacques Rabémananjara	**97**
Lament	99
The Seven-stringed Lyre	100
Flavien Ranaivo	**101**
Love Song	102

Bemin my nie	103
First Fruits	104
Regrets	105
Carry Me Away	105
Dox	**106**
Traveller's Tree	106
Baobabs	108
Elie-Charles Abraham	**109**
I Belong to Tana	109
Esther Nirina	**111**
Prose Poem	111
Thomas Rahandraha	**113**
Appeal	113
Henri Rahaingoson	**116**
The Attractions of Oblivion	116
For a Departure	117
Cacomania	118
Serge Henri Rodin	**121**
Dog Sun	121
Untitled	121
Élie Rajaonarison	**122**
Wake Up! We are All Dead!	122
Message from My Children	123
David Jaomanoro	**126**
Anything Special This Morning?	126
Dina	127
Vololona Picard	**129**
Eve Reading	129
Children not Listening	129
Veromanitra Razafiarivony	**131**
Madagascar	131
A Book	131
A Poem Reflecting My Life	132
Jean-Luc Raharimanana	**133**
The Habit of Writing	133

A Crematory Poem	134
Ndrivo	**135**
Tattoo Art	135
Tombo Ravalihasy	**137**
Pretty Face	137
Lazawell Andriamiariseta	**139**
"Get Up! Stand Up!"	139

SEYCHELLES

The Nanny Who Wanted to Marry (traditional)	143
Antoine Abel	**144**
Your Country	144
What You are	144
The Old Lady	145
A Bat	146
Forgotten Land	147

COMOROS

Aboubacar Saïd Salim	**151**
Salaam Réunion, Salaam	151
Moroni my Sorrow	152
Mahamoud M'Saidie	**155**
The Sign of Water	155
Interview	155
Saïndoune Ben Ali	**157**
On the Beach	157
Getting Round	158
The Whores of Mutsamudu	158
Down There	159
The Four Winds	159
Salim Hatubou	**161**
And So	161
Kamaroudine Abdallah Paune	**162**
Voyage	162
My Somali	163

Death to Immigrants	164
Nkosi Johnson	165
Amir Mounib	**167**
My High-prowed Sailing-boat	167
Adjmaël Halidi	**168**
Evening Prayer	168
Notes	169
Water like Gold / O Comoros	169
To be a Comorian	170
Bitch of Comoros	171

MAYOTTE

Abdou S. Baco	**175**
To My Father	175
First Love-letter	176
Moussa Abdou	**178**
How to Endear Yourself to a Young Maiden	178
Nassuf Djailani	**180**
A Season in the Comoros	180
Yazidou Maandhui	**182**
The Pawpaw	182
The Dream of a Naartjie	183
Dawn at Pamandzi	183

ISLAND REPORTS

Mauritius: From Dodos to Jumbos	187
Réunion: Landfall for a Stopover	191
Baudelaire Rounds the Cape	196
Cruising Off-shore	201
Promenades on Mayotte	214
Two Weeks in Tana	222
Acknowledgements	229
Index	231

INTRODUCTION

If one were to arrive at the islands of the Indian Ocean, one would notice that there are no maps.
— Max Jacob (1917)

Words are like eggs; hatched, they have wings.
— Malagasy proverb

Before those words in poems may take off, some cartography.

What is the extent of the poetry of the Indian Ocean African islands? First of all, we should rule some sources out: the inshore islands like the Bazaruto Archipelago off Vilanculos, and the Quirimbas, for the reason that they belong to continental Mozambique; Mafia and Pemba, which are part of Tanzania; and Kenya's Mombasa Island, Patta and Lamu – so we disregard a piece like Jonathan Falla's in *The London Magazine* of February–March, 1995, about Lamu's Swahili songs; thereby we omit also all the poetry of the dhow routes of the Arabic-speaking sultans of long ago; and on along the Somali coast with its oral performances, up to Socotra, which is no longer technically African, but belongs to Yemen. The reason for excluding this chain of inshore islands is that their literary systems are inevitably attached to their adjacent mainland.

Thus we lose important islomane responses to that ancient Sea of Zanj; for example, the post-independence poems about thresholds, like Amin Kassam's meditation on the meaning of Kenya's "Fort Jesus":

Every day you gaze
Gaze
Gaze out at the boundless ocean ...

or Agatha Wangeci's statement:

In Zanzibar I was born,
A country fresh like weeds of May,
With ocean ripples that tap the coast,
Whose pillars dream of Arabian Nights ...

(in "For Zanzibar"; both poems are included in full in *Drum Beat*, edited by Lennard Okola for the East African Publishing House in Nairobi in 1967). We exclude Rui Knopfli's *A Ilha de Prospero* (*Prospero's Island*) about Mozambique Island (indubitably Mozambican), with his own translations from the original Portuguese:

The fortress sinks in the sea
up to the flanks,
dreaming of unattainable
Moorish vessels.

(See *IZWI*, Number 18, October, 1974.)
  Nor may we include, for that matter, the Maldives, or even Ceylon/ Sri Lanka, which an expatriate Irish poet like Richard Murphy could celebrate as "a tear-drop India shed / On old school maps ..." (Indian Ocean, but not plausibly African).
  The other limitation is a linguistic one. We are interested here in the French language as it is dispersed throughout our region and detached African countries in which French, still today, is the main medium of literary communication, as follows:

	Population	**Square kms**
Madagascar	1 600 000	587 000
Mauritius	1 200 000	2 045
Comoros	700 000	1 300
Seychelles	81 000	455

These figures are quoted in a recent number of *Jeune Afrique* in an article describing the joint activities of the Indian Ocean Commission, which includes within its reach two further territories, both actually up to the present belonging to the French metropole:

Réunion	750 000	2 507
Mayotte	194 000	375

Not all island countries compare readily, either: Madagascar is the fourth largest island on earth, a semi-continent half the size of South Africa and exceeding France in area, while the Seychelles by contrast consists of some 115 islets and volcanic extrusions (the figures vary), with its capital city, Victoria, being the tiniest in the world.

And who has ever taken note of the landfalls sprinkled around them, on a cleavage formed between former continents, like Cosmoledo or Coëtivy Isle, the shoals of Cargados Carajos, the sand spits of Agalega? Or of Diego Garcia in the Chagos Archipelago? – the latter being part of BIOT (the British Indian Ocean Territory, established in 1965), thanks to which its 2 000 Ilois inhabitants were removed in order to make way for a United States Army base to police these waters. And who has heard of their Talipot palm, which produces its spray of flowers only once in eighty years, then expires? And in the contrasting weather of Amsterdam, Saint Paul, Kerguelen and Crozet way down south, where French is spoken when they are inhabited?

In English-language writing knowledge about this region has improved since Daniel Defoe noted "that vast Indian Ocean, perhaps the greatest Sea of the Globe, having very little interruption of Islands ..." But in his circumnavigation of the 1570s Francis Drake missed all the islands after Java, bypassing Table Bay as well (which he nevertheless described as "the fairest Cape we saw in the whole circumference of the earth").

The earliest mention in English of a Cape link with the islands appears in Richard Hakluyt's *Voyages and Discoveries* with the expedition of James Lancaster from Plymouth to the Malaccas in 1591. After putting in at Saldanha Bay and rounding that fairest Cape, they reached an island north-east of Mozambique called 'Comoro', well populated with "Moors of tawny colour and good stature, but they be very treacherous and diligently to be taken heed of." One of the ship's masters, together with sixteen of his men, rowing out for the shore in search of fresh water, upon landing was slaughtered there. (Spellings in English of the modern-day three-island republic vary, but 'Comoros' seems most usual, with the adjective 'Comorian' used to describe its citizens.)

A generation later William Davenant, a royalist and the poet laureate of the British Restoration, was to turn out an epic called *Madagascar*. This was published in 1638 and addressed to one Prince Rupert, nephew of King Charles I:

> And this swift Pilot steer'd unto an Isle,
> Between the Southern *Tropick* and the *Line*,
> Which (noble Prince) my prophecie calls thine …

By which we may understand that this son of Elizabeth of Bohemia was being encouraged by the poet to lead an expeditionary force to Madagascar in order to establish an English colony there. Davenant, in his dream, could foresee the rewards: coral, pearls, rubies, sapphires, diamonds.

While from medieval times Arab traders stretched down the coast to Sofala, with links to the inland kingdom of Zimbabwe, and then extended along the stepping stones of the Comoros Islands to reach north-west Madagascar, they first had come into competition with the Portuguese, who by the end of the sixteenth century had opened the inner passage to the East through the Mozambique Channel and on to India.

It was the Dutch, however, who pioneered the outer passage from the Cape to the East, with Mauritius first being colonised by them in 1638 (and named after Prince Mauritz of Nassau). After 1652 the island became a dependency of the Cape. Our joint story produces many names familiar from the South African history books: one Adriaan van der Stel was the ruler of Mauritius for six years (from 1639) and during that time made three expeditions to the East Coast of Madagascar in search of beef, rice and slaves (the price of a healthy adolescent: one shotgun). His son Simon, by his half-bred wife, Maria Lievens, daughter of a Dutch sea-captain and a Javanese lady, was born in Mauritius and was to become a future Cape governor. The VOC logs of ships for the two centuries after 1600 list, on average, a shipload of slaves for sale transported to the Cape annually.

In the nineteenth century the names of British governors common to the islands and to the Cape become familiar: Sir Lowry Cole, Sir Henry Barkly, Sir Bartle Frere. But it was particularly the competing French merchantmen who opted for the middle passage, taking the East Coast of Madagascar as their refreshment station, like the pirates of the Isle of Sainte Marie before them, and establishing their beachheads there. Recovering from calentures, they had to learn of the Indonesians who had arrived and settled there a millennium before, navigating with star maps made of string. Certainly a complicated pattern of migration and exchange along thin strips of shore.

This was best summarised in modern-day terms by Commodore Owen in his account published in 1833. His title was *Narrative of Voyages to Explore the Shores of Africa, Arabia and Madagascar, performed in H. M. ships Leven and Barracouta, under the Direction of Captain W. F. W. Owen, R. N., by Command of the Lords Commissioners of the Admiralty.* For the purposes of his shoreline survey, conducted over 1822–24, he divided the region into four: the East of the Cape of Good Hope up to the Keiskamma boundary; then along Shakan Zululand to Delagoa Bay and Sofala; the islands nearer the coast including Johanna (Anjouan), Pemba and Zanzibar, with some of the Seychelles, and on to Cape Guardafui and Muscat; and fourthly the circumnavigation of Madagascar, which he and his crew enjoyed for its "laxity of morals", with its numerous dependent isles (like Europa and Juan de Nova).

At about the same time the bones of an earth-bound ratite, the half-ton vegetarian cropper that used to lay eggs eight times the size of those of an ostrich – *Aepyornis maximus*, even vaster than Sindbad's roc – were reaching Europe. It would take an H. G. Wells (in the 1890s) to assemble such a fantastic phenomenon into a work of English literature.

How did this vast, unknown library, mostly in French and intimately connected to South Africa, first become within reach of myself? I was born on the Cape littoral, but facing the other way, with little more than Robben Island in view. But my younger sister arrived and needed a governess, as my parents were often away, and she was to be a certain Nesta Williams, who stepped off the steamboat from Mauritius. She brought her life's collection of books with her, as she had left under a cloud and could not contemplate returning. Nevertheless, her beloved islands lived on in all the tales she told us. In order to understand them, we had to learn her language as well, because those stories she made up were in French, the means of communication she merrily shared with my mother, who had been educated in France. I still have her copy of Michael Malim's *Island of the Swan* (about Mauritius, published in 1952) and F. D. Ommanney's classic *The Shoals of Capricorn* (published in the same year and about wider reaches).

Otherwise, the South Africa of those days was not much interested in any maritime links once the far more important Atlantic had been crossed and the Cape of Storms rounded; that was rather the Suez Canal route to elsewhere. But the vintage travel writer, Lawrence Green, had had the initiative to set out eastwards in 1930 and brought back rumours of solitary Tromelin, named after its castaway sea-captain who left only his name behind, and of remote Réunion being the unwilling home of mighty France's exiles, while *The Outspan* occasionally featured other landfalls no one had known existed, proclaiming them habitable.

In 1950, I remember, Johannesburg's *The Sunday Express* devoted a lavish supplement to the islands, because the French High Commissioner, M. Robert Bargues, was on an exchange visit to the Union over Christmas, while our Minister of Transport, Mr P. O. Sauer, visited Madagascar – South Africa being the colony's third best buyer of exports, particularly of hides (bovine and crocodile). Immediately there followed the biggest newsbreak before heart transplants: Professor J. L. B. Smith's search for that four-legged ancestor, the coelacanth, so that names like 'Mayotte' and 'Anjouan' suddenly fell on everyone's lips; and not to forget his further revelations about other important freaks, like the fur-tongued *Uraspis uraspis*, similarly dredged from the tropical deeps into every South African household.

But it was Tom Bulpin, the Australian settled in South Africa, who in 1958 produced the definitive summary of the region's history and its South African connections in his *Islands in a Forgotten Sea*. Hence tales of blood-money and maroons; the exquisite paille-en-queue, or phaeton, or tropic-bird; privateers and lataniers; mineral springs of chalybate from fumaroles in conoidal lumps; and the Americans really entering the picture now, trading with Majunga (the Place of Flowers) – for live bullocks. With the advent of commercial airlinks, Elsa Joubert was first in with her three-island hop to Mauritius, Réunion and Madagascar in the winter of 1961, as recounted in her superb *Suid van die Wind*.

After the painter Irma Stern had made the iconography of war-time Zanzibar known to South Africans, two other local artists went further afield for inspiration: Alexis Preller was back by 1949, selling canvases of fisherfolk at Belle Ambre in the Seychelles to the Johannesburg Art Gallery; and Walter Battiss made several trips that way, beginning with the Bajun Isles in 1964 and accordingly being moved to verse (in his *Limpopo* of the following year):

Koo She and Aldebaran,
Dschubba and Saiph,
Kursa and Izar,
Phakt and Minkar –
The names of the stars
Sing me to sleep.

Further eye-openers in the 1970s, by which time the islands were on the threshold of the jet age, were the photographic exhibitions of the British-born photographer based in Cape Town, Gerald Cubitt. These culminated in his still unrivalled picture album, *The Islands of the Indian Ocean*, published with a matching text in French by Struik in 1975. By then I had joined the intrepids as well, bringing back the reports collected in the addendum here, in response to a drive for tourists to come from their nearest industrially developed neighbour.

These reports culminated for me in two collecting trips intended to enhance my holdings. The first was to Mayotte (on Air Austral via Réunion) in August, 2005. There I was soon installed in their Bibliothéque Départementale de Pret, or Public Lending Library, in Kavani. Working in the nook of shelves devoted to Indian Ocean literature, I became the centre of an informal network extending by word of mouth, for me to meet writers resident in the environs: the seniors, Nassur Attoumani and Abdou Baco (both employed by the island's Cultural Services), and the up-and-coming hopefuls checking in to exchange their copies of Racine for the latest Houellebecq: Amir Mounib from the Comoros, Nassuf Djailani and the equally wildly talented Yazidou Maandhui, on vacation from France. All of them updated me far beyond what could be recuperated in a trawl through the printed works.

Between interviews and genial social events, then, there were always the back numbers to be scanned, of *Études Océan Indien*, published in Paris, with their Number 17 entirely devoted to the poetry of Madagascar and the Comoros; the University of Madagascar's annual archive publications, and so on. Several authors passing through had deposited signed copies of their works there, too.

The BDP also had the range of recent expatriate and visiting authors' works reporting back on their experiences abroad in these parts (excluded from this project), as well as a full collection of the books produced by those publishers specialising in the written literature of the region: especially L'Harmattan, but also Le Serpent à Plumes, Sépia and Éditions de l'Olivier of Paris, with the new KomÉdit based in Moroni. Almost all their publications were still on sale in the excellent local bookshop, La Maison des Livres (which even then was launching its own imprint, Les Éditions du Baobab). Because this written literature in French, published almost entirely over in France and re-exported back to the new countries, is a recent happening, their target readership is accumulating only slowly. New works accordingly hang around for years, even decades. The first Comorian novel written in the Western style to be published – by L'Harmattan – was by Mohamed Toihiri in 1985; then Abou Baco pulled off the same feat for Mayotte in 1991 – both are still to be purchased. Further, one of the local newspapers, *Le Mahorais*, cordially furnished me with xeroxes of every review they had ever published; and the new *Kashkazi*, with Djailani as its local correspondent and edited in Moroni, was setting out to publish new poems.

One glance at the shelves of publications devoted to recovering the traditional oral literature of the region, especially of Madagascar and with particular mention of scholars like Leonard Fox and Lee Haring, and the decision had to be that that must be another exclusion, in the belief that this editor would never have the extra lifetime required to master such a field with any reliability.

Fortunately I had with me my well-thumbed copy of Carole Beckett's *Anthologie d'Introduction à la Poésie Comorienne d'Expression Française*, published by L'Harmattan in 1995. Remarkably it was the first survey of its kind, conducted thanks to several collecting trips she had made here. My friend Carole's pioneering work became my open sesame, as nothing comparable had been accomplished since and the Beckett benchmark achievement was still widely on sale. When I revealed that Ms Beckett, retired now like me, was a friend of mine of forty years standing, and that she continued to take an interest in promoting that emerging literature, the effect was enheartening.

The biggest run on those shining shelves in the BDP was naturally devoted to the work of, and scholarship on, the founder figure of the indigenous written literatures of the Indian Ocean islands in French, the extraordinary Jean-Joseph Rabéarivelo – the first of them all to become known to English-language readers as well. I had long before attempted to translate some of his poems, not only to keep my hand in, but also perhaps to stir some readers of the then active *Staffrider* with the fact of there being an outsider antecedent whom they might profit from. For he was one who had worked his way through all the Fanonist steps in his career, with utmost application of his genius, well before the publication of Fanon's *The Wretched of the Earth* (in 1961). In the 1920s Rabéarivelo was clearly toiling with Fanon's first phase, that of unqualified assimilation into the literature of the motherland to escape an inferior status; then came phase two, with the memory of his bygone childhood days and the recuperation of old suppressed legends in the light of the new aesthetics; which developed into the third, activist phase of awakening the defeated people, their system of reference liquidated, to revolutionary activity and reclamation of their heritage. Had not Fanon in his "Letter to the Youth of Africa" in 1958 written: "Youth of Africa! Youth of Madagascar! Youth of the West Indies! We must, all of us together, dig the grave in which colonialism will finally be entombed"? And had not Rabéarivelo moved from rimes to tom-toms more than twenty years before?

The magnitude of Rabéarivelo's achievement, and the sheer bulk of the resultant work, would mean having to take courage and face the big one: Madagascar. I had to some extent ticked off the Comoros and Mayotte by then, and had for years been stocking up on material from the Seychelles and Mauritius, mostly on visits to the Africa Centre in London – and for the latter I had also had as a contact Édouard Maunick, resident in South Africa for the last decade.

Réunion, meanwhile, is the most 'developed' and accessible of all these literatures, down even to having its own website ("Lettres de la Réunion" on www.litterature-reunionnaise.org). From that one may readily follow the chronology from 1518 with the first appearance of its craterous landscape and pebble deltas on the map of Pedro Reinal (as Santa Apolonia), through Samuel Castleton in 1613 (Pearl Island), through Thomas Herbert (who left pigs and goats from the Cape there), through Étienne de Flacourt with his *Histoire* of 1648 ... through the abolition of slavery (1848) ... to its becoming a French department (in 1946).

Then in the 1970s begin arising the likes of Axel Gauvin and Jean-François Samlong, the pluricultural figures who are not included here because they are primarily renowned as novelists (as are Ananda Devi and Lindsey Collen in Mauritius), and Carpanin Marimoutou (principally a critic and historiographer). In 1980 the seventh volume of the *Éncyclopédie de la Réunion*, written by Jean Brézé, could be entirely devoted to Réunion literature.

But in 1980, by contrast, as far as the rest of the world could fathom, Madagascar was lost in publishing's outer darkness. Still today Madagascan writers resident on the island tend to preserve their verse in desk-drawers, while those who have some attention paid to their work in periodicals like *Notre Librairie* and *Africultures* are usually based in France (like Jean-Luc Raharimanana and Michèle Rakotoson). Were it not for anthologisers like Jean-Louis Joubert and the indefatigable Liliane Ramarosoa, much of Madagascan literature would never be seeing the light of day. The infrastructure for it has not been developed and, although Antananarivo has six daily newspapers, the few bookshops are practically bare. For a Madagascan poet the only feasible option is to export a collection of poems ... to where else but Réunion, to the admirable Collection la Roche Écrite, published by Jean-François Reverzy at Éditions Grand Océan.

So in May, 2006, I was to have a fortnight in their stacks, courtesy of the Centre Culturel Albert Camus in Antananarivo, established in 1964 and yet the main literary institution of that huge country.

The first creative works from the Indian Ocean region to attract attention outside it were those of the three Rs of Madagascar. Crucially this occurred post-World War Two, in Léopold Sédar Senghor's collection of 1948, *Anthologie de la Nouvelle Poésie Nègre et Malgache*. With its prestigious introduction, "Orphée Noir" by Jean-Paul Sartre, setting the trend, it launched items by poets writing in French mainly from the Caribbean diaspora of Guiana, Martinique (led by Aimé Cesaire), Guadeloupe and Haiti (125 pages), with only three poets – all from Senegal and including the other main figurehead of the Negritude school, Senghor himself – to represent the entire African mainland (with only 40 pages). The Madagascan section was included as an extension of the continent with a further 40 pages, also to be considered as qualifying as 'black', although Senghor's three contributors officially were not Negroes but what today are called Afronesians. These were Rabéarivelo himself (b. 1901), Jacques Rabémananjara (b. 1913) and Flavien Ranaivo (b. 1914), for decades to come the only three names from that remoteness to feature before a Western readership. As Rabéarivelo had concluded his short life in 1937, he could be considered the unheralded precursor, while the two longer lived near coevals, his inheritors of the next generation, were becoming better known, especially through their regular contributions to the movement in the radical black arts centring on the journal *Présence Africaine*, established in 1947 in Paris and still functional today.

In the English-language sphere one of the first figures to champion Madagascan verse was Miriam Koshland. She took from the Senghor, besides several poems of his own, two specimen Madagascan poems, launching translations of them (both included here) in her article published in *Africa South* in early 1960. These the Harlem Renaissance guru, Langston Hughes, had by 1963 taken over into his collection, *Poems from Black Africa*, adding a translation apparently of his own of Rabéarivelo's "Flute Players", which he had previously included in his *An African Treasury* (1960). His editorial decision followed Senghor's that Malgache works should hold a place of honour in an anthology otherwise devoted to black Africans of the mainland, now including some Portuguese-speakers and many English-speakers for the first time, particularly from South Africa's *Drum* school of writers.

When Hughes's *An African Treasury* went into French in Seghers' Nouveaux Horizons series in 1962, Christiane Reygnault produced for them a rich companion called *Tresor Africain et Malgache* (with six Rabéarivelos and three Rabémananjaras). Most importantly, also included was the text of the latter's famous speech made at a conference called to protest the violent repression of the 1947 uprising in Madagascar some ten years before (and first published in *Présence Africaine* in February-March, 1957). There Rabémananjara stated his position:

> The Malagasy are not anti-France. All the Malagasy want is that the French are not anti-Malagasy. Let me put it more exactly: do not make it a condition of our admiration for France that we commit treason to ourselves. Madagascar is our country. Madagascar belongs to us. Her presence fulfils us, just as you are fulfilled by that of France.
>
> Our criticism is not addressed either at the efficacy of Western techniques as an essential factor of modernisation, or at the value or the beauty of French culture as a vehicle of civilisation. It is the malfunctions of that imposed system we attack, those which have

taken on a criminal meaning – those which extinguish, which kill what we hold as the most precious, the most authentic and intimate elements of our very Malagasy existence.

In 1963, a further initiative (in English) was Gerald Moore and Ulli Beier's *Modern Poetry from Africa*. At first this was included in the Penguin African Library (reprinted 1968), and later extended as *The Penguin Book of Modern African Poetry* (1984). Stemming from the Senghor, five items of Rabéarivelo and two from Ranaivo were incorporated there, but in different selections made by the editors, while Rabémananjara was excluded on the perhaps understandable grounds that "his rhetorical, rather long-winded poetry does not translate into English and is difficult to quote shortly with proper effect", an opinion I endorse. Moore (then based in Uganda) and Beier (in Nigeria) in 1963 also further produced a pamphlet of *24 Poems*, published by Mbari Publications in Ibadan: this was the first substantial version of Rabéarivelo to appear in the English-speaking literary world. The only other writer from our region to make it into the Moore-Beier network was to be Édouard J. Maunick, in their 1984 update, with two Mauritian poems taken from *Présence Africaine* and which had been published by them in book form in 1964. These were in fine translations by Moore, marking Maunick's debut in a well-distributed English forum. This sample holds for later anthologisers in French as well, like Jacques Chevrier in his *Anthologie Africaine: Poésie* of 1988 and like Lilyan Kesteloot with the revised edition of *Anthologie Negro-Africaine* of 1992.

Concurrently underway was the team of Clive Wake and John Reed, both initially on the staff of what was then the University College of Salisbury, Southern Rhodesia. Their scheme to highlight the importance of the Madagascan contribution to the general scheme of the developing French-language literature of Africa began with Wake's collection for the Oxford University Press, *An Anthology of African and Malagasy Poetry in French*, which included a very substantial Rabéarivelo selection (nineteen items), three Rabémananjaras and eight Ranaivos, indicating that Wake was intending to echo, but also to broaden, Senghor's representation. When Reed and Wake together put out their first *A Book of African Verse* in the Heinemann African Writers Series in 1964, the three Rs were to feature in a different selection, including what were fresh and excellent translations of the poems which were fast becoming anthology chestnuts: Rabéarivelo's "Flute Players" and Ranaivo's "Popular Love Song" (under another of its many titles). There they held their position through many reprintings, until 1984 when all the Madagascans were suddenly dropped, presumably as being no longer of import as their country sank into a red slough. The replacements were several contributions from South Africa's new 'Soweto' school. This slide from favour had begun in Reed and Wake's 1972 collection, *French African Verse with English Translations* (Number 106 in the African Writers Series), which now reflected the quarter-century dramatic rise of publishing within Africa itself post-1945. Possibly the Indian Ocean islanders were no longer considered exactly 'African' as such, on account of their now being seen as belonging to a potentially separate literary system which could well be elbowed out in favour of mainland Africa's more pressing issues.

But not to ignore the islands entirely, Reed and Wake jointly put out the most substantial study of Rabéarivelo to date, with some 70 pages of his poetry elegantly translated on facing pages, both from the French and also from his Malagasy originals. Their historic effort, called *Translations from the Night* (Number 167 in the Heinemann series), nowadays long out of print, represented the coming into his own of the herald of the literature of the Indian Ocean islands. But there the matter came to rest.

In due course, however, with the rise of programmes of Black Studies, particularly in the United States in the 1970s, the demand for comprehensive anthologies summarising the entire literary heritage increased. Hence the excellent *The Negritude Poets: An Anthology of Translations from the French* (published by Thunder's Mouth Press in New York City), put together by Ellen Conroy Kennedy in 1975. A teacher and a translator herself, she had been nominated for the National Book Award in 1969 for her version of Albert Camus's *Essays*, and could by now assemble a team of some half-dozen further translators who were being encouraged to develop academic careers in this field. Her representation of the big three Madagascans, plus Maunick – who also let her have a poem in admiration of her efforts – is well-informed, not to mention also reads stylishly in English.

The formula that confined the entire literature to 3Rs plus 1M persists unchanged in several subsequent anthologies: for example, in Wole Soyinka's *Poems from Black Africa* (for Secker and Warburg in 1975), where his seven Rabéarivelos and one Maunick appear as part of the African network, without even a mention up front that they are translations; and in Julio Finn's *Voices of Negritude* (New York: Quartet, 1988): two Rabéarivelos, one Rabémananjara and one Maunick, again without the translation factor being noted, although Finn does devote a good introductory chapter to Rabéarivelo's life and work. Now he appears as the "prophecy of the coming of the poets of Negritude", even though by then they were a school considerably dispersed in the world of post-colonial Africa and its Caribbean links, preoccupied with later events. By 1992 even a British poet like Michael Kelly (in *Ambit*, Number 128) had come round to reworking poems by Rabéarivelo and Ranaivo to make statements with them that looked strikingly contemporary.

Indeed, by now 'Negritude' is a term of rather historical interest, having been supplanted by several somewhat tongue-in-cheek successors. In Mauritius in the 1980s the poet Khal launched his 'Coolitude' movement, to insert into the mainstream the voice of the lastcoming population group of the Indian Ocean islands, those who arrived as indentured labourers from India once the slave society had taken on this new form. Receiving wider publicity and general acceptance nowadays is 'Migritude', a neologism replacing the Negro with the name of the world's new migrants, often forced to migrate as refugees. Theirs is the style of the new literatures produced by global displacement in general. Then in Antananarivo I discovered the most international style of them all, thanks to hip hop and rap, etc.: slamitude.

The slam poetry phenomenon there has to be transplanted into French, since it is primarily popularised and carried worldwide in the English-language media. But what of the Indian Ocean countries where their colonial experience has been British, distinct from the French sphere of influence and even, at times, spectacularly at war with it? English-language literature of the Indian Ocean, what little of it there is, may be recuperated readily enough, on account of our own imperial past, at my usual research post – that treasury in the stores of the Johannesburg Public Library.

There I discovered how the Cape periodicals from the 1820s carried regular reports, including poems, from Mauritius and Madagascar, especially with regard to how the abolition of slavery within the Second British Empire affected them in the former with the introduction of the free labour system. In the December, 1848, issue of *The Cape of Good Hope Literary Magazine* the advent of the most recent hurricane to hit Mauritius was promptly recorded, with a lengthy elegiac poem commemorating the loss of the Indiaman George Canning, waiting in quarantine off-shore, with all of her passengers and most of her crew. The poet, merely designated as 'L', could not fail to draw an earlier parallel:

> High on a reef where flowering corals grow,
> And the white waves dash up in wreaths of snow,
> The same fair strand, to which bright genius lent
>   Its mournful tale, – where near Virginia's tomb
>   A cypress stands to mark her piteous doom
> And her fond lover's –

referring to Bernardin de Saint-Pierre's immortal classic of lost love and shipwreck disaster.

In the JPL I also learned that, in the late 1830s, the affable Quaker missionary James Backhouse, with his partner George Washington Walker, toured first the Australian colonies, and then visited Mauritius, Réunion and Madagascar in that order, en route to the Cape, preaching about the progress of evangelising endeavour in the expanding southern sphere as if it were now commonplace. By the 1870s *The Cape Monthly Magazine* used routinely to include English summaries of Malagasy folklore, supplied by the Camerons, representatives of the London Missionary Society based in Madagascar with its regional headquarters in Cape Town.

In the JPL I could locate even the *Journal of the Seychelles Society* of the 1960s, which recorded that the islands had maintained an English-language Literary Society from as early as the 1840s. There I could swot up on factors like these:

In 1903, once the Colonial Office's efforts were off containing the defeated Boers, the Seychelles received the attention it merited and became a Crown Colony, no longer under the political administration of Mauritius. However, not until after World War Two was English decreed to be the only official language to be taught in schools. The first president, when the Seychelles became independent in 1976 – James Mancham – had even published a book of poetry in English, no less (*Reflections and Echoes from Seychelles* of 1972), but most newspapers there remained stolidly trilingual (French and English with Creole). Uniquely in the world, after Mancham was overthrown in a coup d'état, this country of scattered granite bosses, on a submarine plateau situated between 4° and 10° South, declared that the local Creole, called Kreol Seselwa, should be the country's official language and its unifier. In response in 1983 Hazel de Silva, also publishing as Hazel Mugot, put out her extraordinary *Sega of the Seychelles* (with the East African Publishing House in Nairobi). A monologue delivered over 314 pages, this momentous work is in the voice of a preliterate local girl, seduced and abandoned by her 'bouledoux' (sweetheart) and left with the 'bebe' (offspring). Her complaint ranges far and wide, including the history of this Île d'Abondance as seen from below, praising the bravery of its fisherfolk and enjoying its Garden of Eden-like natural wonders.

The flow is intercut with quotations from the popular dance form of African origin, the sega, making a satirical commentary. Her memory proceeds in scraps of English with French borrowings, all following local grammatical formulations. A sample about the capital:

Rue Victoria before
pleine with pousse-pousse
pulled by straining men
now camion rushes by
now the streets
full with people
now the camion
sway with its load
of voyageurs
falling out of
windows and doors

old men beneath
sang dragon trees
they do talk like that
they do say the dress
of the young girl today
too court

trop serre serre
they prefer
the flow
of jupe
embroidery of peignoir

I will go
to the sea shore
to collect la mousse
to give mon ptit bebe …

Such a virtuoso poem continues in this salmagundi fashion, expressing the true feelings of the people more closely than any linguistically unadulterated work would have done. But this is a performance piece, virtually untranslatable into Standard Southern.

The country's first novel was published two years later (bilingually

Kreol and French), with Antoine Abel having by then established a name as a poet (in French) and as an oral poetry collector. More recently the Seychelles-born Maggie Faure-Vidot has made her mark as an oral performer – not in Britain or elsewhere in the Commonwealth to which she belongs, but in France.

The work of the burgeoning international Creole movement must also perforce be beyond the remit of the present collection, with one early item collected by Ommanney as the sole exception. During the colonial period up to the 1960s the word 'Creole' had been taken to refer to inhabitants of French descent resident in the islands, usually the 'grands blancs' class of property owners, but more generally to any of the island-born, even those of slave origin. In the post-independence milieu the term has undergone a dramatic shift of meaning, currently being applied to that patois or pidgin language actually spoken as a lingua franca by most of the population. In the Mascarenes Creole-language writers have been able to claim nineteenth-century antecedents and devote themselves to sorting out the bedevilment of different orthographies. For an early survey of this literature, see James C. Armstrong's "Recent Developments in Creole Literatures on Mauritius and Réunion" (in Volume 11, Number 2, of *Ba Shiru*, published by the University of Wisconsin at Madison in 1980).

In another early survey of Mauritian literature, contributed by Michel Fabre to *World Literature Written in English* in the Autumn of the same year, he pointed out that, despite the fact that English continued to be the new country's official language, only 0.3 per cent of Mauritians usually expressed themselves in English in everyday life, while 4.75 per cent chose to use French (with 53 per cent in Creole and 31 per cent in Hindi). Traditionally the language of the cultural elite, French had remained since the days of Napoleon the choice of the majority of Mauritian writers, thanks to its prestigious appeal of Parisian sophistication, while English in the post-independence administration was still considered more suitable for political works and commercial dealings. While the fact is that French has stricter norms and less syntactical flexibility, and making mistakes in it can imply racial or social inferiority, for a figure like Maunick the appeal of attaching to an existing movement of black writing in French from the old colonies was obviously preferable to having to create an equivalent from scratch in the English he resisted.

Before Maunick was quite a tradition to build on as well: for example, there was Léoville L'Homme, similarly a man of colour, born in Port Louis in 1857. Although he never left the island and was a Protestant, and he knew well enough that French had been forbidden in official communications and the law courts in Mauritius under the British administration since 1847, he could be a journalist like his father before him (founder of the newspaper, *Le Mauricien*) and adopt and adjust the Parnassian style of the white Creoles of Réunion as a counterblast to enforcements of conservative Browning and Tennyson. When L'Homme sang of his Belle Creole, you may be sure that her colour was 'brune' (brown). Insistently he became the first ever poet of any of the Indian Ocean African islands, published locally, to achieve a modest renown abroad.

In 1952 Ommanney, writing of the continuing solid achievements in French of Robert-Edward Hart and Malcolm de Chazal, could also comment that "the local paper, *Le Mauricien*, has only four pages, but it devotes a higher percentage of its space to the humanities than can be found in the vast acreage of the principal Johannesburg papers."

Much of that space would duly be encroached upon by the Creole. Take as a sample a current singer like Patrick Victor of the Seychelles, who can broadcast a song like "Get Together, People of the Indian Ocean":

> Whether you dance the sega
> Or you dance the moutya,
> Whether you dance maloya,
> We are all brothers ...

His choruses are in turn in Kreol, in Réunion Créol and in Mauritian Créol, with a verse in Malagasy. And the overall style is not English but – French!

By May, 2006, then, the assembly of this book has become a committed project, with Jérôme Bessière of the French Institute of South Africa opening the way and Nicol Stassen of Protea Book House in Pretoria expecting results. I am first in at 10.00 a. m. when the CCAC in Antananarivo opens its doors to the crowds of borrowers of their massive holdings, and of students completing projects, rushing for seats. Dominique Chelod is the chief librarian and from her I am privileged to have my own office space, plus that compiler's essential tool, a xerox machine that functions. Dominique introduces me to Pierre Maury, French poet, who immediately publicises over the air the purpose of my visit: I am collecting French-language Madagascan Literature, past and very much present, for the purposes of an anthology.

Soon enough I meet another visitor to their offices, Serge Henri Rodin; he duly instructs the pick of his students to make appointments and present me with sample printouts of their (invariably unpublished) poems. Mamy Yves Rakotomanga, in charge of the mediatheque, becomes my right-hand man. Courteously he organises that I should meet the leader of the Sandratra group (Élie Rajaonarison), more usually over at the rival Cercle Germano-Malagasy; that I should be welcomed at the Havatsa-UPEM office (by Henri Rahaingoson), where I receive copies of yet more work, ancient and modern. There I become a sort of honorary member and regular, qualifying for cut-price lunches. And then on to the next engagement that Mamy has fixed.

The biographical details of all these kind acquaintances, eager to escape the confines of their country now that at last it is emerging from decades of frightening backwardness, are to be found in the headnotes above the examples of their work. As Mamy remarked of his recent past, nothing may become more isolated than an island. Repeatedly, as a white South African also with a limited recent past, I was invited back to the next great Malagasy literary kabary (get together): the 70th anniversary of the death of Jean-Joseph Rabéarivelo, to be commemorated in June, 2007.

To which I could only reply that my interest must remain primarily that of my South African English-language readers, for whom I would caper about translating only whatever I felt strictly capable of attempting (with Carole Beckett as my safety net) ... and then producing, rather than some monumentally representative compilation featuring the entire spread, only what I felt instinctively as a fellow poet might be of interest to us, to serve our own literary interests.

Ah, South Africa with its Spar right opposite the Rabéarivelo High School, converting them all into twenty-first century consumers faster than any diplomacy. When I departed from Antananarivo the check-in (Airlink) would not let my suitcase through, bulging as it was. I had to fly with the excess piled high on my lap.

To summarise, our stress here is solely on the organising principle of that post-imperial world which has come to be called the 'Francophone'. This term embraces the entire French-speaking universe numbering some 400 million people, while excluding the French mainland itself (58 million). The French sphere of influence, we know, stretches from Québec across to Vietnam, and in Africa from Morocco right down to the Congos, and from the West to Djibouti. Mauritius and the Seychelles, despite being for so long British possessions, must be included, because French as the vehicular language of their cultures has persisted there. The concept of 'Francophonie' at present also conveniently overrides distinctions of racial origin, so that so-called 'white' writers may be readmitted to areas once considered uniquely 'black' or, at a push, 'Asian', as has been the case in upland Madagascar for decades.

By 1979 the journal, *Modern Poetry in Translation*, edited in London by Daniel Weissbort, for its Winter Numbers 37-38, acknowledged all the above by launching a whole double issue devoted to the Francophone poetry of Africa; this included, however, only one Indian Ocean island poet – Ranaivo, with his perpetual "Simple Lover's Song", translated yet again, this time by Paol Keineg and Candace Slater. A later issue of *Modern Poetry in Translation* in 1983 included David Gascoyne's extensive version of the prose-poems of Loys Masson, the French Surrealist (who had been born in Rose-Hill in Mauritius in 1915, but never returned there). Traces of his tropical childhood resurface in hallucinatory takes like this (in "The Solicitor Skylark Finds Three

Poems at the Bottom of his Glass"):

> A shark, Emmanuel, wandering around the site of a shipwreck, had inadvertently swallowed a draught-board. He died as a result of the exhausting games of draughts his heart and his liver at once started playing in his innards ... The tide flung his dead body up on a shore where there lived reddish seaweeds and great women like lamps who remained virginal when married.

By the time of the Sixth European Poetry Festival, organised by the Association from the Promotion of Poetry in Leuven in 1984, the work of Rabémananjara could be firmly on the agenda, as a product of the Francophone rather than of Negritude, while the figure of the 'métis' or half-caste, Raymond Chasle, could also be admitted, with some valiant versions of his work made into English by Jennifer Gage. Born in Mauritius, he was soon to be representing his country in Brussels at the European Community headquarters – and besides that, an early exemplar of the new wave of concrete poetry in French. Examples of his work have not been included here on the premise of sheer untranslatability.

As it turns out, several other items beyond the old 3Rs plus 1M have also defeated my attempts, but should be listed. For example, there are the performance poems of Stefan Hart de Keating, nephew of the Grand Old Man, which include catchy rimes and offbeat rhythms difficult to render in English, like:

> Le blanc et le noir sont complémentaires
> Sans commentaire
> (White and black are complementary
> Without commentary);

or the driving satires of the rapper from Rodrigues Island, Joseph Collet, otherwise known on the platform as 'Azazel', who can stomp out:

Voici l'histoire d'un négro sans pesos
Hn! Hn! É KÉ É sale gosse
Voici l'histoire d'un negro sans pesos
Hn! Hn! K roulé sa bosse
(Here's the story of a negro without a bean ...)

This is Francophone literature taken to the outer limits, where it becomes virtual English anyway.

What is included here is arranged as follows: first is a sample of the 'international' authors responding to the Indian Ocean African islands as a single collective idea, the region of our study. Then follow the component parts, with Réunion in the lead, as it has the oldest continuous, indigenous French-language writing tradition. Closely thereafter comes Mauritius. Madagascar must be included next, being the largest section, primarily covering the twentieth century and culminating in the present day. In the order of their achieving independence, the Seychelles and the Comoros follow, both then first becoming known for their literary productions. To fill in the map, finally there is Mayotte, which detached itself from the Comoros in the mid-1970s to remain French and so is the lastcomer. But even Mayotte provides work as accomplished as the output of its extraordinary fellows, all of whom together comprise the poetry of the Indian Ocean African island basin.
    Let it fly.

STEPHEN GRAY
Johannesburg, 2008

NOTES ON TRANSLATORS

The editor wishes to express his appreciation for the work of the following:

Dorothy S. Blair was born in England in 1913 and came to South Africa to lecture in French at the University of Cape Town, soon finding herself at the University of the Witwatersrand in Johannesburg, where she became known as the first in the country to specialise in French African literature. In 1958 she was responsible for the translations of the 3Rs comprising the Madagascan section of Peggy Rutherfoord's anthology, *Darkness and Light*, while in the second of her articles on the Negritude poets (in *Contrast*, Number 3, of Winter, 1961) she devoted most of her space to Rabéarivelo, including the one translation reproduced here. In 1966 she guest-edited a special issue of *The Classic* (Volume 2, Number 2) devoted to Francophone literature and thereafter became widely known as a translator of key works.

Roy Campbell (1901–57), the Durban-born poet, whose *Adamastor* volume of 1930 established him as an important practitioner of verse. In later life, particularly from when he settled in France, he augmented his income as a translator into English, notably of a very complete version of Baudelaire's *Les Fleurs du Mal* (published in London in 1952).

Edward Davis taught English at UNISA in Pretoria and was the professor and head of English at the University of Port Elizabeth. An early one of his many influential contributions to *The South African Opinion* was this translation of the Baudelaire poem understood to be about the Cape (in 1935).

Described as a lecturer, broadcaster and writer on African poetry, **Miriam Koshland** was one of the first to present Indian Ocean poetry to South Africans in English. Her "The Poetry of Madagascar", including the two translations here and several other items, was carried in *Africa South*, Volume 4, Number 2, in January–March, 1960.

Joan Neethling lectured in French at the newly established Rand Afrikaans University (nowadays the University of Johannesburg), where she became professor and head of department, specialising in African literature written in French. Her versions here were undertaken for *Rapport* and for *IZWI*.

Wilma Stockenström began publishing slim volumes of her Afrikaans-language poetry in 1970 and has recently produced her *Selected Poems* (in both Afrikaans and English versions). In the early 1970s she was one of the editors of *IZWI/Stem/Voice*, for which the translations here were done.

All other translations are by the editor, **Stephen Gray**, with one by Carole Beckett; except where sources of previous publications are given, they were all made over 2005–06 for the purposes of this volume.

These fresh translations have all been monitored, with utmost care and expertise, by **Carole Beckett**, based in Pietermaritzburg, where she is retired from the local university's French Department. To her much appreciation and heartfelt gratitude.

Jacques-Henri Bernardin de Saint-Pierre (1737–1814) was born of a noble family at Le Havre, in Normandy, France. After a military training, he travelled widely in Europe and the Caribbean. He was despatched as the king's engineer to the Indian Ocean in 1768, landing in June at the Cape and receiving hospitality from Governor Rijk Tulbagh, whose domain he toured. Based as state botanist in Mauritius, and later on in Réunion, with a brief to investigate the potential of Madagascar as a future French colony, he reported back his findings on the nature and the inhabitants of the places he visited to correspondents in France in elaborate open letters. Subsequently these were gathered and published as his *Voyage* in 1773. An English version, translated by John Parish in London, appeared two years later as *A Voyage to the Island of Mauritius, the Isle of Bourbon, the Cape of Good Hope, etc., by a French Officer*. A friend of Jean-Jacques Rousseau, he also published in 1788 his romance, *Paul and Virginia* – about the tragic love of the two naturally educated youths of Mauritius – which is the foundational text of Indian Ocean literature in French. The item translated here was attached as a postscript to his letter from Port Louis, dated 25 April, 1769, and has often been reproduced as a separate piece, subtitled "Reflections on Slavery" – see, for example, Elisabeth Audouin, *Bernardin de Saint-Pierre et La Réunion* (Paris: Magellan, 2004). He died after a distinguished literary career back in France.

Reflections on Slavery

I don't know if coffee and sugar are necessary to the happiness of Europe, but I know well enough that these two crops have brought misery to the other half of the world. We have depopulated America in order to have land for planting them; we depopulate Africa to have a nation to produce them.

We say that it is in our interest to cultivate the goods which have become necessary to us, rather than to buy them from our neighbours. But while the shipwrights, the builders, masons and other European labourers work in the open air here, why are there no other White workers? And what would become of the present landowners? They would grow even richer. An estate-owner may take it easy with twenty tenants, yet he is poor with twenty slaves. Here one reckons there are twenty thousand slaves who have to be augmented annually by an eighteenth of their number. In this manner the colony left on its own would destroy itself within eighteen years; never mind that it is true that there is hardly any population at liberty to own property, and that injustice is a poor housekeeper.

They say that the recently established Code Noir works in the slaves' favour. Should do: but the harshness of their masters exceeds the permitted punishments and their meanness cuts back on their nourishment, their rest and the rewards that are their due. And if these unfortunates wish to lodge a complaint, to whom may they complain? Their judges are often their original tyrants.

And one may not keep these slave people down, they say, except with great severity: it takes corporal punishment, iron collars with triple locks, whips for flogging, blocks to which they may be attached by foot, chains which clasp the neck; they need to be treated like animals, just so that the Whites may live like humans ... Yes, I know well how once one has established a very unjust principle, one draws from it the most inhuman consequences.

Nor is it enough for these unfortunates to be victims of the avarice and the cruelty of the most depraved of men; they have also to be the playthings of their owners' sophistry. The theologians assure us that, by imposing an earthly slavery, they are ensuring spiritual freedom. But most of them are bought at an age when they are too old to learn French and the missionaries never learn their own languages. In addition to which, those who are baptised are treated exactly like the rest.

They add that they deserve heaven's punishment merely for having once sold one another. Is it for us to be their executioners? We should leave the vultures to destroy the kites.

Politicians have excused the business of slavery, saying that it is justified by war. But the Blacks are hardly able to agree. And if one is convinced that human laws permit it, then one should at least confine oneself to the boundaries they prescribe.

Yet I am deeply angered by those philosophers who argue against all abuses with so much courage, but hardly ever talk of the slavery of Blacks, except to joke about it. They approach it from afar. They talk of Saint Bartholomew's Day or the massacre of the Mexican Indians by the Spanish, as if such crimes are not also of our own period, with half of Europe taking part. So is it worse to wipe out people who have different opinions from us all in one go than to keep on torturing an entire race because we need it for our pleasure?

Those beautiful colours of rose and of flame in which our womenfolk dress, the cotton-wool with which they pad their skirts, the sugar, the coffee, the chocolate at their luncheons, the rouge with which they set off their purity – all these were prepared for them by the hand of a poor Negro. Sensitive ladies, you cry in the theatre over tragedies, while those who actually serve your pleasure are drenched in tears and stained with the blood of mankind.

The mulatto **Alexandre Dumas** pére (1802–1870) was the prolific novelist and dramatist, son of a Frenchman and a Negress, Marie Dumas, and most renowned for his *The Count of Monte Cristo* and *The Three Musketeers*. Fascinated by the topic of slave revolts in the Indian Ocean French colonies, which he never visited, he did however write the historical novel *Georges*, about a half-caste rebel leader, and published it in a magazine serial. The definitive text of *Georges* was not assembled until 1974. The following song was performed during the course of the action at a hideout of runaway maroons by a character called Antonio the Malay.

A Free Man's Song

1
In my little hut I take my rest,
I have to bend to enter there;
If my head hits the roof, best
Stick to the floorboards, never fear.
With evening when I want to sleep
Me, I have no need of lamps,
'Cause just when all the moonbeams steep
I don't lack holes, so God give thanks.

2
My bed is a plaited mat and rug,
My pillow a plank of whitest wood,
A calabash serves as my drinking-jug
Where I keep arrack all year round.
When my wife economises sure
On Saturdays when's finish the rations,

I cook for myself with cow manure
Bananas grilled on all the ashes.

    3
Without a key's my cabin-trunk,
Because I never close it;
Made of bamboo without iron lock,
Who would try to steal it?
If Sunday all's pass without kak
I buy, if I'm not so broke,
To fill my pipe a wad of twak
And watch it all go up in smoke.

Charles Baudelaire (1821–1867) is the leading mainland French poet of the mid-nineteenth century and an acquaintance of Leconte de Lisle. His well-known voyage to the Indian Ocean African islands is described in the addendum here. Over a dozen of his poems in his most famous collection, *Les Fleurs du Mal* in various editions of the 1850s, deal with this youthful experience, just as several of his prose-poems do. The translations into English made by Roy Campbell included below were first published in 1952 as a tribute from a fellow East Coast roisterer and bon vivant.

Invitation to a Voyage

    Picture, my little one,
    Under another sun,
A heaven quite humble, a paradise where
    Days, as this day has done,
    Will flow till our sands are run,
And nights like the nights that inhabit your hair.
    Days like our olden days,
    Smouldering golden days,
And nights showering down from strange hemispheres,
    Will be the warp and woof
    Of our twin lives aloof,
Rich as the tapestries under your tears.
There nothing thrives but flowers of ill,
Lovelily, lazily, sterile and still.

    Soft with antiquity,
    Dark with iniquity,
Subtly will gleam the gear of our room.

    Flowering frailty
    Will mingle exquisitely
The breath of slow death with its odorous gloom.
    Carven deliciously,
    Cunningly, viciously,
Ceiling and mirror and indiscreet screen
    Will whisper us wearily,
    Secretly, eerily,
Of the lovers and sorrows and sins they have seen.
There nothing thrives but flowers of ill,
Lovelily, lazily, sterile and still.

    In our heaven-haven deep,
    Sevenfold-laden, sleep
Ships with their vagabond canvas unfurled.
    Command them, and they will leap
    Cargoes of dreams to reap
From the seven high seas and the ends of the world.
    Aye, and each day will close
    Soft as a sleeping rose,
Delicate petals of purple and gold,
    On the rivers and meadows,
    On the cities and shadows,
On all the small heaven our hungry hearts hold.
There nothing thrives but flowers of ill,
Lovelily, lazily, sterile and still.

(Translated by Edward Davis, *The South African Opinion*, Johannesburg, 10 July, 1936)

Exotic Perfume

When I, with eyes shut, on warm autumn eves,
The fragrance of your warmer breast respire,
I see a country bathed in solar fire
Whose happy shores its lustre never leaves;

An isle of indolence, where nature raises
Singular trees and fruits both sweet and tender,
Where men have bodies vigorous and slender
And women's eyes a candour that amazes.

Led by your scent to fairer climes at last,
I see a port of sails, where every mast
Seems weary of the labours of its cruise;

While scents of tamarind, blown here and there,
Swelling my nostrils as they rinse the air,
Are mingled with the chanties of the crews.

(Translated by Roy Campbell, in his version of *Les Fleurs du Mal*, 1952)

Man and the Sea

Free man, you'll always love the sea – for this,
That it's a mirror, where you see your soul
In its eternal waves that chafe and roll:
Nor is your soul less bitter an abyss.

In your reflected image there to merge,
You love to dive, its eyes and limbs to match.

Sometimes your heart forgets its own, to catch
The rhythm of that wild and tameless dirge.

The two of you are shadow, deep and wide.
Man! None has ever plummeted your floor –
Sea! None has ever known what wealth you store –
Both are so jealous of the things you hide!

Yet age on age is ended, or begins,
While you without remorse or pity fight.
So much in death and carnage you delight,
Eternal wrestlers! Unrelenting twins!

(Translated by Roy Campbell, in his version of *Les Fleurs du Mal*, 1952)

To a Creole

But you lady if you were to voyage with me
would conquer the old world of decay by storm
there is no way those stiff madams could ever be
equal to you in content and outward form

once I've seen your eyes open toward the veranda
and your fuzzy head beckon over your arm
once I've seen your every magical splendour
and touched my fingers on your well-oiled palm

I understand why cyclones hush around you
why roofs batten down as pale lovers sue
and the warm pressure inside turns me over too

for there is no body other than yours
no neck no skin no rind of dress on other whores
that knows why I thunder and come true.

Aan 'n Kreoolse Dame

In daardie geurende land, songestreel,
het ek, onder 'n baldakyn van bome tot karmosyn ontbrand
en palms wat loomheid op jou oë ween,
'n Kreoolse dame ontdek wie se sjarme onbekend was.

Haar gelaat is bleek en warm; die bruin verleidster
het 'n aristokratiese grasie in haar kop se houding;
lank en slank stap sy soos 'n jagteres,
haar glimlag vredig en haar oë selfversekerd.

As u, edel dame, na die ware land van glorie
op die oewers van die Seine of die groen Loire sou gaan,
sou u sekerlik statig genoeg wees om ou herehuise te tooi,

sou u, in die skadu van priële gehul,
'n duisend sonnette laat ontkiem in die harte van digters
vir wie u heerlike oë slaafser as u barbare sou maak.

(Vertaal deur Wilma Stockenström en Stephen Gray, *Rapport*, 22 April, 1973; en *IZWI*, Johannesburg, Nommer 16, 1 Junie, 1974)

The Albatross

Becalmed out of their depth on a bored swell
the sails wrung out and stiff as their shirts
the creak of the rigging and the foggy bell
their chant low from where it hurts

they lassoed in an albatross poor guard
of our night crossing planer of air

on deck like a stricken lopsided bard
his wings like oars beyond all repair

and some poked with a pipe-stem at his eye
some stroked his yellow bill and asked why
he looked so fallen did he miss his sky

and such railing laughter each time he lifted
a streamlined foot and slewed over and shifted
down the hatch and could no longer fly.

Die Albatros

Net vir die pret vang die bemanning soms
Albatrosse, reusagtige see-voëls,
Bedaarde metgeselle van hul reis
Wat die skip oor diep waters agtervolg.

Hul plaas hul neer aan boord en dadelik
Word hierdie hemel-koning swaar en skaam,
Laat jammerlik die groot wit vlerke sleep;
Soos roeispaanblaaie hang dit langs hul sy.

Bevleuelde reisiger, hoe swak, hoe lomp;
Hy, op sy dag so fraai, hoe lelik en komiek.
Een terg sy snawel met 'n vuil, stomp pyp,
'n Ander, hinkend, boots die mank voël na.

Net so die digter, nes dié wolke-prins
Wat op die stormwind sweef en boogskutters verag,
'n Banneling op aarde, uitgejou,
Wat struikel oor die vlerke wat moes vlieg.

(Vertaal deur Joan Neethling, *Rapport*, 17 Augustus, 1975)

Raymond Radiguet (1903–1923) is the prodigy of French letters who came to prominence after World War One as the exemplar of the new tough, unembellished style. Although in his short life he never ventured out of France, his mother was a Colonial Creole born in Martinique. Together with his intimates, the South African poet Beatrice Hastings and the author Jean Cocteau, he planned an elaborate stage spectacle based on Bernardin de Saint-Pierre's novel, *Paul and Virginia*, which was intended to lampoon the supposed prelapsarian innocence of France's dependencies in the Indian Ocean. Little of the libretto survives, apart from this wistful lyric.

Paul and Virginia

Oh God, these stinking colonies!

A disturber of nests, you see,
a bird without wings,
what does Paul get up to now he's alone?
And where on earth is his Virginia?

With You on high, where she need never show her things.

For him and for her,
That planter's fetid atmosphere –
For fair young Virginia and for her lovely Paul –
Used to be their parasol.

(*Staffrider*, Johannesburg, Volume 11, Numbers 1–4, 1993)

Assane Y. Diallo was born in 1938 in the former French colony of Mauritania on the West African coast and has been considered the successor of Senghor. His first collection of poems, *Leyd'am* (*My Land*), was published in France in 1967. His poem below is datelined 'Tana, 1988', after a visit to Madagascar, and first appeared in *Présence Africaine* (in Number 147 of July–September, 1988). The masters of the isle are clearly the 3Rs of Madagascan poetry, with the line "the sails of the dawn" being a quotation of a Rabémananjara title of 1957 (*Les Boutriers de l'Aurore*). Diego is the port of Diego Suarez, nowadays Antsiranana; Mahajanga is often still referred to as Majunga; and Toamasina was previously Tamatave. 'Lamba' is the local name for the East Coast skirt drapery, with another key word – 'valiha' – meaning the stringed bamboo instrument with a delicate guitar-like sound. For the traveller's tree, see later.

Island Words

Beautiful island
from the pages of poets

there are three
the masters of the island
and their opening syllable
is stained by their ancient heritage

island of fragile words
full of overlapping dreams

of Eastern paddles
rosewood and sandal

words hankering with exile
Nosy Be crowned with coral
words forgotten since
the sails of the dawn
Diego, Victoire have torn their anchors
words reborn from cyclones tamed
Mahajanga, Toamasina
hesitant words entangled
with children's laughter
ylang-ylang, zozoro
or the suggestive arabesques
under the corolla
of a bulky lamba
valihas in harmony

Along the footpath
a sign:
the traveller's tree.

(*Staffrider*, Volume 11, Numbers 1–4, 1993)

RÉUNION

Évariste Desiré de Forges Parny (1753–1814) was born on Réunion Island of one of the leading white families. Sent to Rennes in France aged nine to further his studies, he became a guards officer to King Louis XV. Family business recalled him to the island in 1773, where he began writing the poems published as *Poésies Érotiques* in 1778. Nine years later, after voyages to India on French Company business, and notably to Madagascar, he produced his twelve *Chanson Madécasses*, or Madagascan songs. These are held to be among the first prose-poems published in French. In the advertisement for them he noted that "they were collected and translated directly from indigenous sources", in order to give metropolitan readers a sense of Merina usages and customs. He was admitted to the French Academy in 1803 and awarded a state pension. In the mid-1920s the composer Maurice Ravel selected and set some of these for voice, cello, piano and flute. He included the slyly anti-colonial "Fifth Song", which caused a famous uproar at its premiere performance.

First Song

Who is the king of this territory? – Ampanani. – Where is he? – In the royal house. – Conduct me to him. – Are you coming without arms? – Yes, I come as a friend. – You may enter.

Greetings, Chief Ampanani. – White man, I return your greetings and I'm preparing a good welcome. What do you seek? – I come to visit your territory. – You're free to walk about and inspect wherever you please. But darkness is falling and the time to have supper approaches. Slaves, place a mat on the floor and cover it with large banana-leaves.

Bring rice, milk, and the ripest fruit from the trees. Come in, Nélahé; let the most beautiful of my daughters serve this stranger. And you, her young sisters, make the meal cheerful now with your dances and songs.

Second Song

Belle Nélahé, lead this stranger to the house next door; spread a mat on the ground and cover it with leaves to make a bed; then let the wrap which encloses your young attractions unwind. If you notice in his eyes an amorous desire; if his hand searches for yours and he draws you slowly towards himself; if he says, "Come beautiful Nélahé, let us pass the night together"; then seat yourself on his knees. May his night be happy, may yours be pleasing; and don't return until the moment when daybreak permits you to read in his eyes all the pleasures that he will have tasted.

Fifth Song

Do not trust the whites, inhabitants of the shore! In the time of your fathers the whites arrived on this island; we said to them: "There are fields, let your wives cultivate them. Be righteous, be good and become our brothers."

The whites promised, but meanwhile they went back on their word. A menacing fort was built; thunder was concealed within the mouths of their cannon; their priests wished to give us a God which we could not recognise; in the end they talked of obedience and slavery: death, rather! The carnage lasted long and was terrible; but, despite the lightning which they vomited, crushing entire armies, they couldn't exterminate us all. Do not trust the whites!

We have seen new tyrants, stronger still and more numerous, planting their tents on the shore: the skies have fought on our behalf, hurling down on them all rains, storms and poisonous winds. They are no longer there, and we are alive and we live on free. Do not trust the whites, inhabitants of the shore!

Sixth Song

Ampanani: Young prisoner, what is your name?
Vaïna: I am called Vaïna.
Ampanani: Vaïna, you are as pretty as the first ray of dawn. But why do your huge eyes let such tears escape?
Vaïna: O enemy king, I have had a lover.
Ampanani: Where is he?
Vaïna: Perhaps he died in the battle; perhaps he had to save himself in flight.
Ampanani: Let him flee or die; I will be your lover.
Vaïna: O king, have pity for the tears which wet your feet!
Ampanani: Then what do you wish?
Vaïna: That poor man kissed my eyes, he kissed my lips, he slept on my breast; he is in my heart and nothing may tear that out of me …
Ampanani: Take this veil and cover your charms. That's settled.
Vaïna: Permit me to go and search for him among the dead, or among the fugitives.
Ampanani: Go, beautiful Vaïna; perish the barbarian who would please himself ravishing you with kisses mixed with your tears.

Ninth Song

A mother dragged her only daughter along the shore, to sell her to the whites.

"O my mother! Your womb carried me; I am the first fruit of your loves: what have I done to deserve slavery? I've comforted you in your age; for you I've tilled the soil, for you picked the fruit; for you I declared war on the fish in the river; I've protected you against the cold weather; I've led you during the heat to the fragrant shade; I've watched over your sleep and shooed the nuisance insects from your face. O my mother, what will become of you without me? The money you'd receive wouldn't give you another daughter; you'd be destroyed by poverty and my greatest sadness would be not being able to assist you. O my mother, do not sell your only daughter!"

Fruitless plea! She was sold, burdened with fetters and led on to the ship. She quit her dear, sweet homeland forever.

Eugène Dayot (1810–1852) was born of a commercial family in Saint Paul where he attended school before departing for Madagascar to earn his keep. Aged twenty, he returned from there to Réunion, suffering from leprosy. Nonetheless he managed to found a literary journal called *La Créole* and to conduct other literary activities. A complete edition of his poems with several other descriptive writings in prose was published in Saint Denis in 1977.

To Colas
(Cook of my Uncle A –)

Farewell, poor Colas,
Farewell, tomorrow alas!

You'll look for me everywhere
And I'll not be there.

Don't cry, for this I know:
All finishes here below;

Each pleasure, worry, little fear,
All will slowly disappear.

Even you will cease
At the hour of your release;

Then you'll quit against your wishes
Your kitchen and your dishes.

But Colas, please don't feel,
When we're at the final meal,

With all your little ways
You, whom I so praise,

No matter the weather,
My footsteps leading wherever,
That I'll forget you ever.

(Written at Terre-Rouge, 28 May, 1835)

I the Leper

If ever snows of age were to bleach my head,
Would I still have a soul and to whom would it overflow?
No, hapless one, at the port where abandonment waits instead,
Without joy and any regret, I'll have ceased to know!
No child on the threshold of endless days
Will ever receive my paternal embrace!
Gasping in bed, fighting my agonising end,
Vainly I'll search for any lady friend!
In this world, where everyone born must live and die,
What will I leave? Nothing, not even a memory!

(1836)

Thanksgiving

Thank you, brother, thanks, for your voice so blessed;
Your sweet-sad chant, as it reaches me,

Revives in my spirit, sceptical and depressed,
    A poetic belief.

Yes, thank you, but alas! on this sacrilegious day,
Shattering my lyre, shocked by my labours in vain,
I quite forgot that poetry must alleviate
    All human pain.

I forgot in this world where the cold blast devours
After eternal struggle the miserly harvest,
The muse with her tender accent disempowers
    Us of our deceit.

What faith, my God, when destiny destroys
With brutal blasts our dreams of a future? –
Like fruits aborted by hope's lies
    As they mature.

You have said the poet must not moan and mope
For he receives from on high the gift to sympathise;
To dying Lazarus he gives the hope
    That he'll arise.

Just as the cyclamen, flower of dreamy folds,
Over the fields unwraps itself to disperse,
So the poet, when his heart bursts and unfolds,
    Exhales his verse.

Here below he should accomplish his holy mission:
A Christ of charity, of the intervening word;
Before God he must explain the sadness of each position
    And mean to be heard.

Yet, like Esau, all my holy heritage
I've sold off to satisfy my yearning.
Madness! Is not desire just a page
    Endlessly turning?

In my bitter chalice are honey-sips of worth,
Harvest of your pious pacifying and my mother's care;
Prayers and love, the pure incense of earth,
    Are welcomed everywhere.

But should, behind my back, the Saviour in his ire
Move to reverse my sad days and nights of dreariness,
Poor resigned Job, I'd retrieve my lyre
    To charm away my weariness.

And what if they're lost, all my forgotten glances,
A future exchanged for a less sombre past?
I'd love to sing for you of all those youthful dances
    In a voice that would last.

Thus I'd sing of that Creole maiden,
Proud and fiery hearted, her eye bright as the sky above,
Her suave smile, her words sweetly laden
    With her first love.

I'd sing of our beloved isle outdoors,
Its envious ocean, its fickle affairs
When love caresses her, or when the fury roars
    And smites her unawares.

I'd sing of our forests, our deepest ravines,
Our jungle of palms forever greenly alive;
Our waves of flood, with terrible scenes,
    Crushing all in their drive.

I'd sing then of our peaks, our proudest height,
Of our volcano built by each eruption;
And of our caves without end, trademark and delight
    Of all our tradition.

(1847)

Charles René Marie Leconte de Lisle (1818–1894) was born in Saint Paul to a well-established professional family. He spent his youth shuttling between Réunion and the motherland, with a particularly memorable stopover at the Cape in 1837. In 1845 he finally left the island for France, where he became known as a radical republican, utopian socialist and spokesman for the anti-slavery lobby. He was the chief founder of the neoclassical Parnassian movement in French poetry in the 1850s, establishing rigid formalism as the style with successive volumes (*Poèmes Antiques* of 1852, *Poèmes Barbares* of 1862 and *Poèmes Tragiques* in 1884), all of which remain in print in popular editions. In 1886 he was elected to the French Academy. In 1977 his ashes, together with those of his wife, were disinterred and sent to Saint Paul where they were reburied in the coastal cemetery. Several volumes commemorate his connection to his birthplace – for example, there is Idriss Issop-Banian's *Leconte de Lisle: Un Poète Créole et son Île* (Saint Denis: Azalées, 1995).

The Palanquin

In the haze as pure as muslin frill
    Every Sunday morning
You came to town in a rattan palanquin,
    Over the slopes of the hill.

The bell of the church gave a lively tinkle,
    The sea-breeze lulled the cane;
Like a shower of gold, on the headlands of the plain,
    The fire of the sun twinkled.

The bracelet on your wrist, the ring on its golden claw,
   The scarf on your chignon,
Carried by two Telingas, your regular minions,
   You were on a litter of Manila straw.

Bending their knees, braced and nervy but singing a tune,
   Supple in their whitest jackets,
The bamboo on their shoulders, hand on plackets,
   They strolled along the lagoon,

Across the causeway and down the wooden paddles,
   Where the old Creoles were smoking,
And the group of merry Negroes, toking
   To the sound of Malagasy fiddles.

In the heady air floats the scent of tamarinds;
   At large over the swell, brightly lit,
In immense draggles and loops, the birds split,
   Diving into foggy, salty winds.

And while your little pink foot, sliding out of its slipper,
   Hangs over the edge of your sedan,
In the shelter of leafy ebony and the litchi fan,
   I see the crimson lips of such a tripper,

While a butterfly, the two wings fully blown,
   Tinted with azure and hectic endocrine,
Poses for an instant on your most delicate skin
   And leaves there a heightened tone,

One notes through cambric drapes a neat surprise,
   The buckles of your pillow gilt,
And feigning fatigue, beneath their lids' half-tilt,
   The gorgeous amethyst of your eyes.

That's how you arrived, on each sweetest morning,
   From the hills to attend High Mass,
With naive grace and your rosy youthfulness,
   Your panting Hindus under the awning.

Now, in the sterile beach of our sandy sea,
   Under the scrub to the sound of the ocean,
You rest with all the dead so dear to mention,
   O charm of my earliest fantasy!

(1845)

The Palm-tree

Slender palm,
Airy tree,
Whose green branches
Fan-shaped,
Flutter in the wind,
Pouring out,
Whenever the sun
Yellows the sky
The pure drapery
Rounded,
Which from afar
Catches the view
Of an extended
Blue without end;
Oriental,
Original,
Even wonderful!
So mellow,
So gracious!

That the wind caresses
With only a sigh
Of sweet pleasure …
Of gracefulness
And haughtiness,
Free, ventilated,
Your sheath soars up
And sways
With pleasure
And noble grace
To refresh
Whoever passes!
And then also
Like a pitch of gold,
Like a prestige,
Shining, fluttering,
Illusion
And fiction!
The wing in flames
And contracted
Of the cardinal bird,
Red spiral,
Like the foliage
A bit flighty!

(1837)

Malay Pantoum

The lightning shoots its crooked arrow,
To the horizon waves are streaming.
On your bark mat, fine and narrow,
Your eyes half closed, you keep on dreaming.

To the horizon waves are streaming,
The thunder glares over the spume.
Your eyes half closed, you keep on dreaming,
Inside the house which you perfume.

The thunder glares over the spume,
The shadow's a prey to howling sleet.
Inside the house which you perfume
You dream on and smile, my sweet!

The shadow's a prey to howling sleet,
Lost in the depths of a mountain ravine.
You dream on and smile, my sweet,
A plain heart filled with songs divine.

Lost in the depths of a mountain ravine,
Among the bustle of a water-spue,
A plain heart filled with songs divine.
Embark, head for the breaking blue!

Among the bustle of a water-spue,
A tree shakes out each branch and beam.
Embark, head for the breaking blue,
On the wing of an amorous dream.

A tree shakes out each branch and beam,
The leaping rock is torn apart,
On the wing of an amorous dream
Cradle up your burning heart.

The leaping rock is torn apart
Where the drunk seas split and harrow.
Cradle up your burning heart!
The lightning shoots its crooked arrow.

Song of the Negro Fisherman

A bird sings and beats its wings,
The wind awakens on the horizon;
The transparent, frail cup
Where the butterfly sips
A heavenly tear which quivers
On the edge of a flower, a sunbeam!
Already the front of the isle reddens
Under the eye of morning, sweet chief!
O my pirogue, carry me well
Over the blue and changing swell.

The shore is a real paradise
Shining beneath their dawn!
The coconut trees rise boldly,
And under the shade of a sycamore
Where the palms cluster around
Sweet fragrances are soon released;
But those I love less than you
Of the breaking wave, my nimble gazelle!
O my pirogue, carry me well
Over the blue and changing swell.

Carry me far from this land
And all its hateful memories,
Because on the lonely ocean,
Overwhelmed by its harsh spell
And filled with boastful bravery,
I may sense the coming of liberty!
Here I live! And in my servile heart
The divine spirit banishes all fear.
O my pirogue, carry me well
Over the blue and changing swell.

The lively fish are still to be found
Along the coral, their red retreat;
Go, pirogue, while they sleep
Beneath the azure of silent ripples,
Before their golden fins
Are disturbed in all this clarity.
Do not alert them now,
Crawl like a crafty serpent.
Over the blue and changing swell
O my pirogue, carry me well.

The shore has vanished into the haze,
The silvery veil of fresh morning;
Over there, the mountain lights up …
A wreath of foam spurts adrift,
Fringing the salty billows
Under the keel of tamarind!
The choppy wave wrinkles and flies,
Hunted by whites I flee the law …
O my pirogue, carry me well,
Over the blue and changing swell.

Soon the larger dinghies will lean
Their white wings on the horizon;
A sad and touching remembrance
As those dark sea-swallows,
Towards the scarlet of dusk,
Transport me back to my home shores …
Youth, love, O sweet trust!
Were they only a sterile fancy?
O my pirogue, carry me well
Over the blue and changing swell.

But no, alas … I'm dreaming!
Life together with freedom

Goes well enough on one's home ground,
Under the fine sky which had to be left behind;
But between us a wall was built,
A wall of bronze – immensity! –
And now I've only a fragile arm …
O my companion, all I have is you,
O my pirogue, cradle me,
Over the blue and changing swell.

Quickly, hook out for the white man
That golden fish sporting
Beneath the surface, shining mirror!
Quick, throw the line, heart atremble
As my hand shakes it down
And my cheeks burn with shame;
On both sides terror roars at me,
Even ashore and on this tranquil sea:
Over the blue and changing swell
O my pirogue, cradle me.

A bird sings and beats its wings,
The wind awakens on the horizon;
The transparent, frail cup
Where the butterfly sips
A heavenly tear which quivers
On the edge of a flower, a sunbeam!
Already the front of the isle reddens
Under the eye of morning, sweet chief!
O my pirogue, cradle me
Over the blue and changing swell.

Stray Dogs

The sun on the waves had drowned its flames,
The town was asleep beneath hazy mountains.
On the great rocks washed with frothy spume
The sombre sea rumbled down its huge breakers.

The night multiplied its long lamentation.
No star glittered in the naked immensity;
Alone, the pale moon, opening the clouds,
Like a mournful lamp swinging sadly.

A secret world, marked with signs of rage;
Debris of a dead globe scattered by chance,
From its frozen orb it lets loose
A sepulchral glow on the polar ocean.

Beyond boundaries, to the North, under sweltering skies,
Lies Africa, hidden in thick shadows and fog,
Its famished lions prowl on smoking sands
And resting near lakes its troops of elephants.

But on this arid beach, with its unhealthy stench,
Among the bone remains of oxen and horses,
Skinny dogs, scattered, lift their muzzles
And bay, sending forth their sad howling.

Their tails curved under panting bellies,
Eyes dilated, trembling on their feverish paws,
Cowering here and there, all howling, motionless
Except every so often for a rapid shiver shaking them.

The sea foam is smeared on their backbones,
Their scraggy coats let their vertebrae stick out:

And when the tide rises in bounds to assail them
Their white teeth snap between their red chops.

Beneath the wandering moon of ghastly splendour,
What unknown distress, on the rim of black tides,
Makes a soul cry out in such an unclean way?
Why do you grieve so, terrible spectres?

I do not know; but, you dogs howling on the beach,
After so much sun that will never return,
I always hear, in the depths of my confused past,
The desperate cry of your savage suffering.

(Cape of Good Hope, 1837; *Poèmes Barbares*, 1862)

Pierre-Claude Georges-François (1869–1935) was born in Saint Denis and made a career as a colonial administrator in Madagascar and in various postings in Africa. His *Poèmes d'Outre-Mer*, from which the two items here are taken, was published in Paris in 1931.

Atlas

The words we don't know
are beautiful for what they conjure up.
O, in the atlas there are
such beautiful names and fine stories!

In those little squares,
green, yellow or lilac,
beside the rivers that they border,
as if a traveller tramps along step by step,
the finger sometimes stops
and a dream takes possession
of a whole country he doesn't even know.

Please, be seated: you're so tired of departures!

The deserts are somewhere there,
and then marshes and lakes reddish with sun.
Rising from the oasis in parallel spouts
under the flaming midday sky,
the long, lean palms, counting the hours,
already turn their shadows around the huts.

Such memories round about your heart.

Do you recall what it was made those marks;
the innkeeper on his doorstep, the ferryman on his bank,
and that haunted forest with its green nightfall?

The friendly barge carried you to the shore.
And the harbours. Do you remember? And the immense seas
and the return crossings aboard those steamers?

I'm sure you remember. You dream, you hold your temple.
You are laden with memories and the night is calm.

And that house, your birthplace. The sweetness of
your island home. The familiar brightness of the lamp.
The appearance of people and of things found once more.

You do remember.
                      The world is infinite.
Life is immense and grand.

But more than in the atlas
and the beautiful geography books,
everything is in you.
                      Everything is in you!

(1931)

At Saint Marie

At Saint Marie de Réunion
under the bridge
the water flows green from the rum distillery.
At Saint Marie the blowers of shells
wait at their baskets of fish.

Don't you love this corner made so pretty
by the pavements
with rows of stalls
where the Malagasies,
the Asiatics, the Blacks take their seats;
by the old church too,
with its door always open
and its shingle of grey moss
and the green moss on its walls?

Wait a bit on the road.
Of all times of day, this
is the special one,
when the flowers of red flamboyants are dropped
in piles on the macadam like flames
and the flames of skies are red like the flowers.

For so long now the clock has stopped at the same hour,
so we're always on time for our rendezvous
with those whom I love to see, close to your heart:
the sea rising and the shadows falling
and climbing like rampant ivy
among the tombs
of the cemetery.

Wait a moment to enjoy this hour
and wait till the aloes and the thorns
turn more blue, darkening in the dusk.

It's the great daily
mystery
which returns
with the enchantment of earth,
on the tracks becoming deserted
further along,

with just enough breath
to believe there's a breeze.

Let's go! a wipe of the handkerchief on the windscreen
and take off your gloves:
you'll feel the vibrations of travel better.
My dear love, there is
the same feeling, the same amount of sentiment,
in departures and in returns:
our life is held between those two moments.
Our life will be immense and deep
enough to spread round the world.

Now there is peace on your face
lit up,
and each evening after all the same scene
for our same as usual promenade.

Let's return to town where doubtless
the servant girl,
in her faded cotton bodice,
will already have lit the lamps
on the veranda.

Great branches of trees wave their adieu,
a moving carpet,
the sombre sea, the blue sky,
these white perfumes
of flowering ylang-ylang,

and then nothing, a passer-by, and nothing again
except for the tiny still lanterns,
the electric eyes of a dog,
caught in the car's headlights …
And there are the first streetlights of town.

Louis Ozoux (1869–1935) was born in Saint Denis and qualified as a medical doctor. A volume of his verse was published posthumously in Paris in 1939. The satirical poem included here occupied a central place in the trendsetting anthology, *Les Poètes de l'Île Bourbon*, published by Seghers in 1966, which established Réunion as a longstanding and influential source of Francophone literature.

A Dionysian Evening

The leafy cinnamon-tree droops its heavy greenery
On the brooding pediment of the old mansion.
In the distance the ocean drags out its orison;
The gloomy sky fogs up the heavy scenery.

Under the pale glimmer of a lamp with a history
The veranda overflows from a hot exhalation
Of jasmine; geckos on the ceiling make demonstration
Of their carnage of airy insects, their venery.

In the swinging Indian chairs with downcast dreariness
Where the evening rocks their musing and weariness,
The couple without children languish, abandoned.

And all of a sudden in the prodigious silence
From the nearby crossroads the night-watchman with violence
Twice yells out his cry: nine o'clock has sounded.

'n Aand in Saint Denis

Lowerryke kaneelbome buig swaar blaredrag
Tot by die ou huis se peinsende fronton
Daar ver sleep die oseaan sy gebed
Oor duister lug beweeg 'n donker wolk.

Onder die bleek lig van die hanglantern
Druif warm jasmyn-asem oor die stoep
Gecko's wat jag verslind teen die plafon
Gewigtelose gogga's, hulle prooi.

In seilstoele, soepel en verstelbaar
Wat saans vermoeienis en drome wieg
Kwyn, stokalleen die kinderlose paar.

Uit die reuse-stilte styg daar skielik
Vanaf die hoek langsaan die wag se stem
Hy roep tweemaal; dis nou nege uur.

(Vertaal deur Joan Neethling, *Rapport*, 17 Augustus, 1975)

André Cazamian (1876–1944) was a further Saint Denis-born poet and lived as a science teacher. His "Native Isle", dated July, 1938, demonstrates the growing awareness amongst its practitioners of a literary tradition in formation. His work features prominently in the second major anthology of Réunion poetry, the *Grand Livre d'Or de la Poésie Réunionnaise d'Expression Française des Origines à Nos Jours* of 1990. The predecessor poet mentioned, Antoine de Bertin, was a lush lyricist whose dates are 1752–1790.

Native Isle

Antoine de Bertin and Parny the knight,
Brothers in arms, bound by their birth-place
And their golden lyre honouring a live Eros,
In our young morn, tuned their voices aright.

Propertius or that Tibullus, brightest Latin light,
Inspired them – and so, in their endless verse,
We have Cynthia, Thetis, Eléonore still worse,
With their lips all of coral and breasts so white.

But the heart does lighten to evoke such an isle,
Yes, even one so far from the Bois de Boulogne,
Paying court to Creole beauties of their very own,

And for each secret hour, adoring their exile,
In the luminous shade they'd taste their sweet bonbon,
Aside the Indian Ocean, under the palms of Bourbon.

Boris Gamaleya was born in 1930 in Saint Louis and lived in exile in France for twelve years. Since his return to Réunion in 1972 he has published several volumes of verse. A sample of his work is included, with an English translation by John Taylor, in the *Revue Noire* of March–April, 1995 (Number 16). The following tribute is from his *Le Fanjan des Pensées* of 1987, the whole collection being dedicated to the memory of his Madagascan forerunner. The reference to the Arab's White Ox is to Rabéarivelo's poem about the Southern Cross, "Le Boeuf-blanc", in the volume *Presques-Songes* (1935).

To Jean-Jacques Rabéarivelo

the mother land
    O Rabéarivelo
the dear land
reborn from the death brought upon you
and more than the assassin
you suffer in your soul
the high land up here
has not finished with
the spleen of the day
quaffed to its source
a charming valiha melody
drifts over
   Imerina
and the sea disperses you
over the skies of our archipelago
and through you we are united
in the south further than south
where the Cross

                    merges with
the Arab's White Ox so light
in the eyes of the lunar land
that we believe we can see
                              the bird
pulling off the leaves in the forest
                                  the extending verb
of our eternity

In his early twenties, **Alain Belair** (born 1953) self-published a pamphlet of poems in Saint Denis (in 1975). Called *Causement Comèla* (*Things as They are*), it made game of highflown, proper French-language verse. Five items from there were reproduced in the issue Number 41 of *Contrast* in December, 1976, with literal, word-for-word translations by Christabel Grare. He was born an orphan and took to creolising mainland French early on for satirical ends.

Lil' French Paradise

Here's Réunion
Just like la France
We listen to same songs
In this lucky lil' département

Others says la France is nice
But Réunion is a paradise
Take a look how the sun shines
Here it's packed with lovely girls
Besides, one peep and they come
Even from very far
If you've got piles of dough
Don't hesitate, make a tour
Come here to spend a vac
Réunion is also part of la France
You'll pick up our patois easy
Besides, there's no great difference

Absolutely you'll find a hotel
And see how easy life can be

No need to bash your brains
Here you'll just let go
If you need to bronze up on the beach
Or hit the trail of lovely mountain

Up there flies the beauty tropic-bird
In the dunes are only lovers
Our town crawls with people like ants
Scuffling after grains of rice
Try and swop idea with us
On this lil' French isle.

Up There in the Bush

Me, I have a lil' straw cabin
It's up there in the bush
Me, I put in table, bed
I go buy curry and rice

It's jolly in my cabin of straw
Specially up there in the bush
Even without the telephone
Me, I play my gramophone
I don't have a spirit-stove
But I cook my food in oil

No need to fear the rain
In my cabin you'd sleep quite well
In my cabin not one mosquito
I chase them with my swatter
In the bush it's really nice
Lots of room on the straw-mat

Come listen to the blackbird calling
On my mat you'll dream …

If you're afraid to get up late
For alarm I have cock-crow
You'll gobble all your dreams with honey
Then warm yourself in the sun
For sure you'll never regret it
Often you'll walk round naked.

Die Vrou, die Man

Alain waar is
Brood vir die kind
Hy moet melk kry
Ek moet geld hê
Die ganse dag
Loop jy maar rond
Met nooiens lol
Jy soek geen werk
Om kind te voer
G'n rys in huis
Die lig gesny
Kerrie is klaar
Dis nou misere, daai
Die kind raak maer
Kos moet hy kry
Heelnag huil hy
Hy's siek sê ek
Alain ek trap
Vat my goed gee pad
Ek kan nie aangaan nie
Daar is g'n water selfs

Luister my skat
Sien my oë traan
Die lewe is mos swaar
Vir arm sukkelaars
Oral soek ek werk
Kantore ver en wyd
Huisves vet niksnutse
Maar het g'n werk vir my
Net waar ek gaan haal ek
My hoed vir hulle af
Daar is g'n werk vir my
Verlaat ons dan tog nie.

(Vertaal deur Joan Neethling, *Rapport*, 17 Augustus, 1975)

Claire Karm was born in Toulon (in 1958) but was educated in Réunion, where she has published work consistently since the 1980s. The poem here first appeared in a journal called *Ti-Kabar* in 1989. She is one of the island's few women's voices and a literary personality of great distinction.

Last Postcard

The bridges over the poetry pool must grow longer
Because
The ocean extinguishes itself, is short of scope, lacks life
    The poets are bricked in
They're short of, short of desire

They lack, they lack that rush of speech
O Island do we celebrate you yet again or drown?
   I'm going to, I'm going to go into reverse, my face veiled
      laugh to capacity
With the fools of the far rocks and flee
      Flee at last
They've lost, they've lost their desires
Like one caressing a cheek
flesh to flesh
To sculpt a handful of sea ...

MAURITIUS

Robert-Edward Hart de Keating (1891–1954) was born in Mauritius of Franco-Irish ancestry. Although he made numerous translations of English texts into French, and throughout his life was a British citizen, he wrote his own work exclusively in French. With over forty publications to his name, at home he was considered the major literary figure of the first half of the twentieth century. For a while he edited a local review called *Zodiaque*, in the 1920s, and worked for a newspaper, insisting that he contribute abroad as well (for example, to the review *Latitude Sud 18°* in Madagascar). Generally his policy was that any colonised reader should resist being a mere consumer of metropolitan culture, learning to adapt it to serve his own purposes. Towards the Second World War he became renowned as a hermit, living in a house he built out of coral on a cliff-edge, overlooking the ocean near Souillac; currently it is preserved as a museum. In English studies his career has been overlooked, with the exception of Michael Malim's travelogue, *Island of the Swan*, where the appendix is entitled "The Poetry of Robert-Edward Hart." His "We're Closing" is from his volume written during the war – *Plénitudes*, published in 1948, shortly before his death. Many later Mauritian poets have paid tribute to Hart – for example, Eddy J. Changkye in an issue of *Les Cahiers de la Mer Indienne*, guest-edited by Édouard Maunick (in Port Louis in 1959).

We're Closing

    The end of the world has begun.
We have killed off the past
Without creating the future,
Brought the caveman back to life
In the laboratory where
Planetary death is germinated.
– Why flower, rose? Nightingale, why sing?
Why then – O verbena – give yourself the trouble
Of embalming the fragile garden?
All's provisional and utterly condemned.
Why flourish – O young girl –
And shake in the wind your sunny head of hair?
O pale adolescent, flesh for cannons, there is
Legal slaughter of large lads from in front,
So why trouble to learn your Greek
And the art of building your own hearth?
    The night without stars is coming, the tides of dark
Unfurled beneath the funeral gods
Of the Tribe, of the Fatherland and of Mortuaries.
Under the leafless trees
Sombrely they return,
All the crows in mourning.
The cathedrals are shaken,
They sense the coming of the wind of death
And the Acropolis may only mock
For it is no longer protected and the sombre silk
Is marked with a secret sign.
Perhaps Chartres will collapse on our heads.
The Parthenon has been notified ...
Since man is more cruel than the outrage of time.
And over the sepulchre of Christ
The bomb with its grand emptiness insults.

This is the time of scientific savagery:
Attilas of the university, atomic Tamburlaines.
This is a good time to die,
To achieve the end silently
Because the human voice may no longer win
Over the deadly trump of this Jericho.

(*Staffrider*, Johannesburg, Volume 11, Numbers 1–4, 1993)

Malcolm de Chazal (1902–1981) was born in Mauritius to a family already established there in Bernardin de Saint-Pierre's day. In his youth he worked in the sugar industry. After publishing several notebooks of philosophical thoughts and aphorisms in the 1940s, he was hailed by the Surrealists in Paris as a unique, untutored genius and eccentric, whose enigmatic prose-poems enjoyed a huge vogue. Several of these were translated into English by Irving Weiss in the 1970s under the title *Sens-Plastiques*. In 1974 the great anthologiser and editor of Indian Ocean literature, Camille de Rauville, compiled a further selection of his polemical and mystical writings *(Chazal des Antipodes)*, with a preface and afterword by Léopold Sédar Senghor. His large scenic paintings, done in the naive style, are known throughout the island and elsewhere to this day. The following mock-serious piece is extracted from a supposed tourist guide he compiled in 1973, asserting an origin myth of the islands which had been invented as a variation on the Atlantis story in the 1920s and has held sway ever since.

Lemuria

All the primitive history, folklore and legendary knowledge of Mauritius is dominated by one fact: inscribed on clay tablets found on the plains of Indus there is the rumour of a lost continent which once filled the basin of the Indian Ocean, stretching eastwards towards the Pacific, and which to the west was detached from Madagascar but joined up with Patagonia and South America. To the north, this continent was attached to what is nowadays called India.

This proto-ancient continent was known as Gondwana on the

plains of Indus and as Mu in the Far East. The occult archives of the West talk of it as: Lemuria.

So once upon a time there was a civilisation established at the base of the planet in the Southern Hemisphere, which in prehistoric times disappeared owing to a cosmic catastrophe. One theory, established by Professor Hoerbiger and dealing with the known facts, established that not that long ago the earth had two moons. One of these moons drew nearer to the earth in a spiral movement.

In this manner that moon raised the waters of the oceans, forming a belt at the equator. Consequently in that zone the bottom of the Indian Ocean was open to the skies, while its waters rose right up to the buttresses of the Himalayas. That is why, for example, high in the mountains of Chile one finds landing bays. They signify that the sea rose up to there, beating the flanks of the chain of Andes almost to the summit.

When the second moon tumbled to the earth, the belt of water which formed the equator was destroyed. In collapsing it established the Indian Ocean.

As a result Lemurian civilisation had to disappear. The inhabitants of the plains of the Lemurian continent were drowned, while those living on the high plateau were asphyxiated. The continent itself was submerged under the waters, with the island of Mauritius being one of the few remaining peaks.

Pierre Renaud (1921–1976), of mixed-race parentage, was based most of his life in Port Louis, where he was a noted columnist on *L'Express* newspaper. Although thoroughly bilingual, he chose to use a type of Mauritian negritude to propagandise for the newly emerging African states. He was the Mauritian representative on the editorial board of *Cahiers Littéraires de l'Océan Indien,* the journal published in Madagascar in the early 1960s. He collaborated with the older poet and novelist, Marcel Cabon, to produce various local histories. His survey-essay, "L'Île Maurice a la Croisée des Civilisations", appeared as "A Song for Mauritius", translated by Lucienne Leeb-du Toit, in Cape Town's *Contrast,* Number 31, of July, 1973. His first, and only, volume of poetry, *Les Balises de la Nuit (The Buoys of the Night),* was published in Mauritius in 1974. A later number of *Contrast* (Number 41 of December, 1976) carried three poems of his from there, accompanied by literal translations by Christabel Grare. In the case of "Here are Words", her version has acted as a useful crib here.

Classified Small

Wanted for purchase
a little portable African
guaranteed dependent
do not apply if you
don't know only how to say
yes to the miesies.

Here are Words

here are words as many as you want
make a poem make a song
millrace anemone saffron
mizenmast scabby cucumber
here are as many words as you want
with between the words silences
of blank margins and spaces
here are all the words you want
slip them on a spinning-wheel and spin out a poem
railway-coach sleeper harpsichord
make them dance make them sing
make images in the colour of your dream
make a prayer to measure your pleasure
your pain

here are the words the silences the white spaces
may they sparkle in the full sunlight
may they scan the course of your wanderings
stress syllables and consonants and the gaps
between words
revive the ancestral dance and its secret magic
go back up the rivers and their sources
here are words as many as you want
make them howl groan bawl out
pain solitude wrong love
here are as many words as you want
turn them into flowers turn them into weapons
and then let them be your breath your heartbeat
make good use of them following the best teaching
spit them in the face of those who obstruct you
man's freedom man's grandeur and dignity

or just go on asking their pardon
yes make a great pardon of white flax
with which to embrace those who know not what they do
make a cutting whip of it and be without mercy
or make that great pardon
yes, make a great pardon beaten dog that returns
head resting on the knees of his master

here are words more words as many words as you want
honolulu vancouver bruges of the red bricks
manhattan harlem ouagadougou
turn them into unending leavetakings
for unending returns to yourself
island of red cymbals
words of teleprinters words of neon
words of a thousand languages
words all the way to drunkenness
see that they yield up the last drop
this world the slaughterhouse
make a shield against all civilised savagery
ambulance conflagration famine ten thousand casualties
dawn attack skulls exploded grenades ready to burst
flight panic death flight panic death
the telegram spells out the unnamed deceased

here are words as many as you want
drag them out through the dust of villages
drag them out through the slime of the communal drain
they'll bear flowers when spring returns
in every accent in every language
the words will sing
words living stones
hopscotch ringdove larch
fire march fire march fire

here are words scattered words
in all the meridians
words singing words dancing and crying desperately

here are words
silence them
and lift to your ear
a shell of the morning
in which the silence of the stars lasts
listen without a word to
the deep song of the world.

Édouard J. Maunick was born in 1931 in a village of Mauritius, of the mixed blood of three continents, one of his famous statements being:

> I, the child of all races
> soul of India, Europe,
> my identity branded
> in the cry of Mozambique.

He was the director of the Municipal Library of Port Louis until 1960 when he emigrated to Paris, soon becoming a regular contributor to the journal *Présence Africaine*. One of his pieces there, an open fan-letter written to Miriam Makeba after her appearance at the Olympia early in 1967, was jokingly signed 'Métis Insulaire' (Island Half-breed), and began his engagement with altering the course of South African affairs. Some twenty of his poetry collections include *Le Cap de Désespérance (Cape without Hope)* (1985) and *Mandela Mort et Vif (Mandela Dead and Alive)* (1987). Through the 1980s he was the director of UNESCO's collection of translations of representative works of the world. In 1973 Keorapetse Kgositsile included an English version of his poetry in *The Word is Here: Poetry from Modern Africa* (Maunick being the only Indian Ocean African island poet to be included); in other English versions his work achieved further prominence in the anthology edited by Ellen Conroy Kennedy in its final form in 1989, with his four substantial pieces being translated by various hands. He was also featured in interview in the last issue of *Staffrider* (Volume 12, Number 1, of 1996), collected in *Indaba: Interviews with African Writers* (Protea, 2005). In 1995 he had been appointed Mauritian High Commissioner to South Africa and has since his retirement made his home in Pretoria, where an English version of his *Mandela* poem by Norman Strike was recently published by Protea.

Pro Memoria

I live on the shore to defend my own country
I really need this war
they're old volcanoes plotting a return
and I'm tied to the neutral tide
inclined to be fiery and angry why not?
my words-roots-rebellion surge up
it's not just that I condemn new shoots and fountains
and the pleasures of living with clear indications
but in my guts is a heavy brazier

inclined to be fiery all I'll have to do is repent
I'll begin without let-up the game of the prow
I won't ask for or even expect pardon
all began with my birth
the only trial

I was born on a narrow land
pinched between meridians
crazier than crazy wanderings
and the Island of voyages
from cape to cape and bay to bay
only the distance of escape is unique
there under the sun are the doors of salt
and the barriers to midday dreams

and the Island of voyages the fist hidden for sure

but with portable lifelines and a loud voice
despite the tiny yellow-bellied bulbul
that never stops singing that never stops singing
– O narrow land of legends
pinched between defining seas
nothing will change the voyage
of the beast beneath the Southern Cross.

(1966)

Parabasis

I remember those words between the END and me, all our arguments borrowed from the lone ISLAND. Today once more, they're far from being exhausted: and since then I've discovered other islands. Some of them have come to me like a blow to the heart. Pell-mell Prague Angola Mozambique Harlem Watts Madagascar Biafra Bangladesh Guinea-Bissau Bolivia Léros Londonderry Québec Palestine Oradour Dachau the American Indians ... I know, Death, you find the list too long, you want to change the colour of your eyes without realising that they're always injected with blood. Some other islands of the present and past: Algeria Chile Haiti Rhodesia Burundi Burgos Lebanon and I've forgotten the rest. As for those infinite headlines alongside the sea: Vietnam South Africa ... And suddenly the broken bit: California like a huge cavalcade.

(1976)

From South Africa on the Teleprinter

... during the night a woman
no longer tries to sleep/
she won't sleep again/
she won't wait again for the day/
Moloise is to die/

during the night a woman
unhooks a shirt/
holds it against her skin/
she recognises the smell/

during the night a woman
stops at a table/
examines the objects/
feeling a terrible absence/
Moloise is to die/

during the night a woman
studies her ghostly hands
they no longer know how to touch
the emptiness rubs them out/

at first light/the woman
lost all her heart/
THEY HANGED HER SON.

(1988)

Clifford Ng Kwet Chan, born in 1932, is of Sino-Mauritian ancestry. In 1971 he published *La Condition Terrestre*, while the pamphlet from which the following poems are taken – *Mémoires du Présent* – was released in Port Louis in 1975. His work was welcomed and boomed in the local press by Pierre Renaud and Jean-Georges Prosper.

Mea Culpa

Bless me, father,
For I have sinned.
This very day
In the street I greeted a pimp,
I had a drink with a cuckold,
I returned through the corridor of a prostitute,
I paid a visit to an adulterer
And I chaffed my friends
On the subject of pederasts and of lesbians.

The Dustbins of the Rich

In the so-called developed countries the dustbin is the symbol of wealth. The bigger the property, the more dustbins there are. Even the smallest dwelling is provided with at least one.

And how huge those dustbins are! They are at least ten times the size of the tiny so-called 'sanitary tins' we have here.

Every evening their dustbins, placed on the stairs or in the courtyard, are filled to the brim. The next day they are empty once again because, very early in the morning, the cleaners come to take them and empty their contents into an enormous truck, which departs for an unknown destination.

When will we have such large dustbins into which we may chuck all our surplus food?

Flashback

1

Sorèze. What a pretty name for a small village. An evocative name, full of magic. That name should have been chosen for the title of a film or a romantic novel. How about *One Night in Sorèze,* or even *Last Spring in Sorèze?*

It's a pity that such a pretty name should be mixed up with two criminal acts occurring approximately one month apart. The first was a rape committed in plain daylight and the second the theft of a car. The latter had disappeared one night at Curepipe and was recovered the following morning, stripped of its engine, of its battery and its wheels, at Sorèze.

I don't mind admitting that I don't yet know that corner of Mauritius with such an enchanting name. And what prevents me from visiting it at the moment is the fear of being taken for a malefactor returning to the scene of his crime.

There are some localities the names of which evoke reprehensible acts, just as certain people by their appearance look like jailbirds. Not Sorèze, in any case, the name of which is at the same time a spellbinding music and a haunting perfume.

2

The sight of Tayeb wedged between the reefs the other day made me think that creating a floating nightclub there with gambling halls and sometimes an orchestra, and offering variety shows, would not be such a bad idea. Our warm summer nights are so numerous that we would certainly like to be able to pass a few in unusual surroundings and away from dry land. Even at only a few metres from the coast we would think ourselves very far from our daily preoccupations. Furthermore, it would surely be a paradise ... a sea for high livers, if the whisky and cigarettes were to be sold duty free. Some of them, if that were to be the case, could even choose to take up residence in a permanent fashion, something which would relieve and at the same time resolve the housing problem.

3

If you wish to conclude a business deal with a Chinese merchant on Mauritius, it's useless to go looking for him at home or in his shop between eleven o'clock and one. You won't find him. For him it's the time for 'yam cha' – or for tea, if you prefer.

'Yam cha' is taken between pals, most usually among men. And, because of the large number of dishes served, it has necessarily to take place in a restaurant.

In Mauritius, for this light meal of midday, the Chinese generally take China tea, which they drink without milk or sugar, with a variety of meat dishes which they call 'niuk nian', 'kiao', 'sao maë' and 'pao' (a type of round bread without crust, inside of which is either meat or a sugary paste), then an egg pie and a kind of sticky cake made of rice flour.

The waiter places the teapot on your table, and you yourself have to lay out the cups which, for hygienic reasons, he brings you scalding in a great bowl.

If it's a waste of time looking for the Chinaman at his home at this hour, that is not to say that you shouldn't go and find him in whichever restaurant he frequents. I can even say he would be delighted to invite you to participate in the 'yam cha' and to introduce you to his friends. The atmosphere in which his revelry takes place would be made even more cordial by your presence, because the secret of really appreciating 'yam cha' is conversation.

Especially don't imagine that you'll have less chance of concluding your business. Quite the opposite! With his hunger and thirst appeased, he would be really mean if he raised any difficulties.

By the way, why don't you invite him to a 'yam cha' yourself? In a restaurant saying just those two words would cost you perhaps a dozen rupees. But do you realise how many you'd gain in return?

Jean-Georges Prosper was born in Port Louis in 1933 and has lived as a teacher of English and of French. In 1977 he edited the *Mauritian Anthology of Literature in the African Context* and the following year he published a history of Mauritian Literature in French (with Éditions de l'Océan Indien). As a poet he has been admiring of mainland French, but prides himself on his Creole origins, propagandising for an 'indien-oceaniste' vision. A selection from his six previous slim volumes was published by La Pensée Universelle in Paris in 1973, dedicated to Sir Seewoosagur Ramgoolam, the new Mauritian premier. Both the following poems, however, are from a collection of his of 1964, published four years before independence.

Golden Bird

The best of fruit
has become my flesh.
My veins distil
the sugar of orchards.
I wear a festive raiment
flaunting vitamins.
And my steps on the road
make a song of blue bees.
Yes, I've tasted so many
blue desserts
that my fruit-eating heart beats
only at the mention of more fruit.
I am the living fruitage
of a millenarian poetry.
I have noble blood

I descend from autumn.
My country born of the sun
reveals on the edge of vision
those canes filled with sugar.
I came to earth
to sing of the sun.
I return victorious
from the battle of great winds.
I threw into disorder
the cavalry of the strong winds.
I've conquered the seasons
and chained up the squalls.
The sky has remade its fair solitudes
and the fruit ripens in colourful peace.
So sing, people of the Tropics
people of Earth.
Sing, all sing out
for the sky of ripe fruit.
Sing for the rising sap
so that our labours bear fruit.
Sing of the orchards, cane, the vitamins,
my colourful country, with great kisses of sweetness.

Insula Mea

The wind on the flanks of the mountains blows my island towards I know not which port.
    So float, little island, towards that horizon too far away and too close.
    Float to the limit of sea and sky.
    The clamour of palms sounds like a conch held to the ear on mild evenings and your heart is as living as beating wings.
    Once at Chamarel the gods improvised girls out of those

living clay colours and grew drunk on the moon and music.

People came. The men chose their residence at the foot of your hills; they built their own towns.

But you were no less beautiful, green isle of the Tropics.

Isle of sandy loins and of legends.

For you the sun on the spray is a sheaf of rainbows.

The wind on the flanks of the mountains blows my island towards I know not which port.

Henry Koombes (also known as Ennri Kums) was born in Mauritius in 1948 and is known principally as an artist. For many years he lived in South Africa, exhibiting in Durban, Johannesburg and Cape Town, before returning to Mauritius in 1983. This poem was contributed to the *Revue Noire* issue devoted to the topic of African artists and AIDS (Number 19 of December, 1995 – February, 1996).

The Rictus on an Angel's Face

There it is on every copper we spend
There it is in the ceaseless outcry of orgasm

I see this inkstain in the blue, unshadowy sky
I see the rictus on an angel's face
You sense its odour in a field of roses
You sense it passing in front of a butchery
He hears it in the clockwork of a watch
She hears it in a trap slamming shut
We read of it in Confucius and in Rimbaud
We read it in every glance around us
You breathe it in with the air around you
You breathe it in, in richness or in poverty
Men hear it in each musical note
Women hear it in every battle-cry

The door was wide open,
but
I saw it:
    it entered through the window
And since then
it has made the cover of *The Economist*

    The next day it was seen
        coming out of the president's mouth
And it has raised its colours
        in every court throughout the world.

Carl de Souza was born in Rose-Hill in 1949. After studying biology in London, he became a high school teacher in Mauritius, latterly as the headmaster of Saint Mary's College. He has four French-language novels to his credit and has published short prose pieces in several journals. The following sketch in poetic vein was originally titled "Tamarin: Prends la Vague", after the tamarind trees giving the place its name. It first appeared in *Revue Noire* in March – April, 1995, in Number 16, which was devoted to Indian Ocean Island Literature.

Tamarind Bay

Sketch me a mountain. Not with too gentle slopes. A real one. A sort of dagger, yes, an armament, a flintlock brandished by a mysterious fist thrust from the depths of the earth with the barbaric intention of tearing the sky apart. That's what Rampart Mountain is like, with its summit ravelling out into haze. Isn't that haze in the western sky very dry, pure, almost arid? Not likely, but in my mind the sky of Tamarind isn't blue. Grey sky, brown beach ... That must come from one of those melancholy afternoons when one finds oneself down at the bay without knowing why.

At the foot of your mountain you'll make a stream gush forth. Yes, I know it's not exactly like that, as all those geography textbooks go on repeating. But what matter when, from the beach, the rock and the stream seem inseparable. A burst of water grows larger, loses itself in alluvium and undergrowth, then, having at last decided, it rushes towards the bay. By contrast, on some days it sulks before the sea, this river. Then one may reach the beach with dry feet. The boats stay confined to the estuary, awaiting the water's goodwill. Nor is it always the river's fault. There's another factor, even more bitchy than the river. The sea. Absolutely nowhere else is she more freakish than at Tamarind. For her you will have to choose a metallic, cross-grained tone. When the wind swings to the west, you'll do up her hair in huge rollers, in roaring breakers. By studying her more closely, you will notice that she is pitted with tiny creatures, impudent parasites, swishing about and sniggering. They will have waited whole days for her to get fed up with them. Patiently. Staring at the sides of the sandbanks, the 'spots' with their bizarre, ever-changing names, until their eyeballs pop. Then, deciding all of a sudden, they'll thrust their boards on to the water, straddle them and row out energetically with their arms.

Your eyes sparkle. You're burning to join them on their boards. But me, I'd die of fear to watch you head out for the open sea. But I know it'll have to be. You'll have to leave our beach and in turn take to the waves. When night falls perhaps we'll recognise you as you return among the exhausted ghosts, on your head a bundle of shark-feed, a fishtrap or a piece of driftwood. Drunk with fatigue, you will tell us how wonderful it was, the isle, the reef. Or will you have lost sight of all that in the whirlpool, in quest of even greater waves?

Like the ocean, man has few frontiers at Tamarind Bay. Black or white, with a hairy head scorched by the sun like the Savannah Mountains, ragged clothes. At all hours of the day sleeping off the effects of grass or alcohol, in order to forget some mysterious illness which even the sea does not heal. You get back to nature, lose the measure of time. Tamarind lets you forget that beyond the mountain, if you take that road, life continues.

After that you'll draw me another one. Yes, another mountain, just so that we'll be forgiven because of the first. A sort of hill, if you prefer. Nowadays it welcomes on its outskirts the homes of holidaymakers. This will have to be the Turret. It has been better brought up, these days, tamed by a host of bright plains in flower. Another Tamarind, now charmingly mirrored in the waters of the salt-marsh.

But you should place on the beach, in a corner of the tableau, an old, dark, gnarled stump. Thrown up by the ocean or carried down by the river? Yes, it'll be there, at the meeting place of the sea, the wind and where in my dreams I'd rather like to wait for you. There you'll find me when you return, once you've rid yourself at last of all your demons.

Khal (full name: Khaleel Torabully) was born in cosmopolitan Port Louis in 1956, where his father owned a printing works that produced the daily newspaper, *Le Citoyen*. With a High School Certificate he left for Lyons in France in 1976 where he rose to taking his doctorate in the semiotics of poetry. He has published several slim volumes, including one written in English. His *Cale d'Étoiles*, published in Réunion in 1992, was favourably reviewed by Jean-Georges Prosper in the issue of *Notre Librairie* devoted to Mauritian Literature (Number 114 of July–September, 1993). In their issue Number 128 (of October – December, 1996) he was able to expand on the 'Coolitude' movement, which he leads. Work of his from the same collection was also featured in issue Number 16 of *Revue Noire* of March – April, 1995.

My skin sings

My skin sings more than I can. It's for that that I'm born in a country where one's name is written on the water. My skin speaks more quickly than my voice. It is my true load.

It's because of that that my cries are the undertow of a man caught up in silk, transported for nutmeg and rooted in sugar. By the islands and colonies.

My skin is the caulking of my flesh, of all the memories sustained with the pitching of masts.

My song is thus coolie: my coolitude is my only portion of a memory swept by waves. In the wake of ships which planted men at the end of the world, I wish to express my human freight and my flesh of ink. Because my words watch ships passing with empty hulls.

And if I've chosen

And if I've chosen a ship with strange accents of the sea, it's to be at home everywhere else, even among the words most foreign to my borrowed soul. The doors of the world were battered down for me by navigating with a cooling-of-blood and a drift-of-flesh.

Coolie, because my lost memory chose its roots in my truths.

But I take hold of the language only insofar as it adopts me, so as no longer to be cut off from speech.

And, on the threshold of the French language, I strike out at vowels and consonants differently. Because in the first place I love words more than my injuries.

And I speak my French language to indicate my home port on the map of my discoveries.

In the end it's a marriage between my oceans and my continents.

In Memory of Pierre Poivre of Lyons

(Agent of the French East India Company
and Governor's Intendant on Île de France, 1767–72)

Burn from Albuquerque to Goa,
at the Cape of Storms
without Hope
plunder the spices of the Malaccas,
then shred to bits that book of Marco Polo –
my lateen sail, muslin of wind,

the only exploit that I never made!

Sedley Richard Assonne has been a journalist on Port Louis's morning daily, *L'Express,* and the press attaché of the Social Security ministry there. In the 1990s he founded a movement subsequent to Khal's Coolitude called 'Les Plumitifs Associés', which advocates the performance of poetry in public places. In the *Notre Librairie* featuring Mauritius in 1993 he chronicled the history of the local dance, the sega, and its developments into spoken verse. His own poems are written in Creole as well as in French, with the one below winning the 2003 Jean Fanchette Prize in a competition calling for anti-war items.

He was Called Ali

and he wasn't taller than three apples
juicy ones
exactly as they should be
to give taste to life
he was no higher
than three fruit
plucked from the tree of paradise
to make heads turn
such that life tasted of cider
he wasn't tall enough
too much of a child
to be making war
but still they involved him
in their warrior games
now there are gaps
in the apples

because they dared to trample
over God's orchard!
the innocence of childhood!

MADAGASCAR

The first modern African poet in French, **Jean-Joseph Rabéarivelo**, was born Joseph-Casimir in Antananarivo in 1901, shortly after the French conquest of the land; the hospital building where he was delivered has been converted into the city's present Museum of Art and Archeology. His father was a peasant of ex-slave stock, socially unacceptable to the family of his mother, a Merina aristocrat who had fallen on hard times. After schooling up to twelve years, he became perforce largely self-educated on the post-Symbolist generation of French-language poets and earned his keep as a proofreader in a printshop. He began to publish in his early twenties; when the journal *Latitude Sud 18°* was launched in 1923 by Pierre Camo, he was the first and only indigenous contributor to it (his "Note on the Tribe of Beggars", of an early number in 1924, is characteristic) and took a stand anti-exoticism. From 1930 he became one of the editors of *Capricorne* where, under the pseudonym 'A. Valmond', he placed many critical pieces, including requesting himself to take over Monsieur Valmond's columns during the latter's absence overseas. The bulk of his work could not reach a reading public, however; for instance, he completed two masterly novels about the colonising system as he witnessed it, but these were not to see print until more than fifty years after their composition. As is startlingly familiar to today's many critics and interpreters of Rabéarivelo's work, the fact is that – never having travelled out of his home country and apparently humiliated by being denied a visa to pursue his career in the motherland, and sped on his way by unruly behaviour and various addictions – he committed suicide in 1937. Also well-known is that

he shockingly kept his last journal (reproduced here) as he went. As a precursive, independently African voice his place in literary history became secure once Senghor in 1948 had nominated him first off as the one whom Negritude poets should emulate. Anniversaries of his death became waymarks: in 1957 his reputation was rehabilitated from imperial oblivion with, three years later, a beautiful edition of his French poems published in Antananarivo, still on sale, billed as "translated from the originals by the author"; in 1987 he was declared a national figurehead, and so on. By 1990, furthermore, when Hatier put out the first mass paperback of his poetry, the extraordinary revelation was that he had written almost every poem twice over, first in Hova and then in French, or vice versa, so that his oeuvre is best represented on facing pages. (The story is told in full in *Notre Librairie's* Number 110 of 1992, which dealt with Madagascan Literature in French.) For South African readers he first became known thanks to the efforts of Dorothy Blair (in 1958) and Miriam Koshland (in 1960), with some of their versions of his poems included below. More recently his tomb, pictured here, has become a national monument.

Note on the Tribe of Beggars

At the start of the sixteenth century there lived a man, a chief. He had two sons, one of whom took up the profession of thievery and the other begging. Over many years matters continued like that with impunity, until the day, caught in the act, the thief was arrested and condemned to death.

Once he had courageously pronounced the verdict, the father called all his family together. He held forth to them in the following words: "All of you know now what a sad end awaits this poor child who broke the law; you know, on the other hand, what freedom is enjoyed by the other one, who is content just with receiving alms! And I curse in advance whoever among my descendants does not follow the second one, who is really wise. May he lose everything he gains and have nothing in his life! Because stealing kills, while begging lets you live!"

Since then a whole tribe has formed under the name of Androrosy, which survives even in our day, at harvest time, by beseeching the generosity of the producers with a tearful persistence.

Begging, especially if one is young, robust – even rich sometimes – does not always yield much and for ever! Noticing that people grow tired of seeing them, the Androrosy have worked out a means of being well received: singing and, of course, dancing.

At the present time they have a pretty abundant repertoire with which to vary their performances. Usually they sing nostalgic songs, the form of which remains faithful to the most beautiful old Merina songs, which have four stanzas at most.

The women sing these in all the styles, sketching out a really simple dance, all to do with movement of the fingers and the buttocks, while the men, solemnly, slowly and regularly, beat time with their hands. Sometimes they'll have two empty sardine-tins to click one against the other; the note which these improvised cymbals give out, in harmony with the song, manages to create a really curious musical figure.

But even more interesting is the poetry which gives life to these little songs of the beggars. One may say that they have put all their souls into them and allowed them to foretell all their misery. One may judge from the following quotation, in which they eloquently demonstrate what their nomadic life demands of them in terms of lengthy journeys and adventures:

> Follow heedlessly your road,
> O you first-born of my life!
> Whether you go to Belsiriry
> Or you push on till the west of the West!

"Let us go far, and further still!" The attraction of the unknown!
And here is another stanza:

> What month are we travelling through
> In our life?
> Is it not the month of lamentations?
> The month when you think of those
> Who barely think of you?

Or again:

> Fortune's ship lands for the others,
> But we drown at sea!

So, by dint of begging, even if they're rich – and, I repeat, such cases exist – as these people end up telling themselves, we may believe they are really poor.

Happy is he who can kill what he is and live naively by deception.

Here She Stands

Here she stands
her eyes reflecting crystals of sleep
her eyelids heavy with timeless dreams
her feet are rooted in the ocean
and when she lifts her dripping hands
they hold corals and shimmering salt.

She will pile them into little heaps
close to the bay of mist
and give them to nude sailors
whose tongues were cut out,
until the rains begin to fall.

Then one can no longer see her
but only her windswept hair
like a clump of unwinding seaweed
and perhaps some grains of salt.

(Translated by Miriam Koshland, *Africa South*, Cape Town, Volume 4, Number 2, January – March, 1960)

Your Work

"You have only heard the singing,
    you have only sung yourself;
    you have never heard men speaking,
    you did never speak yourself.

"What are the books that you have read,
    save those conserving women's voices
    and things unreal?

"You have sung, you have not spoken,
    never questioned the heart of things
    so you cannot understand",
    so speak the orators and scribes
    who laugh to see you magnify
    the daily miracle of sea and sky.

But still you sing
    astonished still in thinking of the bark
    which seeks an untraced path
    upon the tideless seas
    and finds its way to gulfs unknown.
    Astonished still you gaze up at a bird

not lost in heaven's wastes
but finding in the wind
the paths that lead back to its forest home.

And so the books you write
   will rustle with the sound of things unreal
   unreal because they hold
   too much of dreams.

(Translated by Dorothy S. Blair, *Contrast*, Cape Town, Number 3, Winter, 1961)

Filao

O casuarina tree, brother of my sadness,
come to us from such a far, ocean-going land,
has our Merina soil also, for your tall slimness,
the favourable element most private to your stand?

You seem to grieve for those dances on the shore
of maidens of your sea, the sand and the salt breeze,
and in a dream you see the stormless morning of before,
your unstoppable sap rising, gloriously at ease.

Now that your exile has caused your bark to crack,
the spurt of green feathers falters, grows slack,
for the birds you offer a hopeless place without shade,

so will my song be a labour foolish and vain,
if, depending on imported rimes and made
rhythmless, it never feeds on the blood of my pain.

(1928)

(*Staffrider*, Volume 10, Number 2, 1992)

Flautists

Your flute,
you fashioned it from the tibia of a powerful bull
and you've polished it on the arid hills
scourged by the sun;
his flute,
he fashioned from a reed trembling in the breeze,
and the holes he made alongside running water,
drunk with moonlit dreams.

You play them together at the heart of evening
as if to hold back the curved pirogue
capsizing on the shores of the sky;
as if for it to be delivered
from its fate;
but your plaintive incantations,
are they heard by the gods of the wind,
and of the earth, and of the forest,
and of sand?

Your flute
draws out the tone, the tread one hears
of an angry bull pounding towards the desert
and who returns pounding
burnt with thirst and with hunger,
but beaten by fatigue
at the foot of a tree without shadow,
without fruit, without leaves.

His flute
is like a reed that bends
beneath the weight of a bird of passage –
not a bird taken by a child,

its feathers all standing up,
but a bird lost from its kind,
watching its own shadow, for comfort,
on the running water.

Your flute
and his –
they regret their origins
in the songs of your sorrows.

(*Staffrider*, Volume 10, Number 2, 1992)

Tall Trees

I have not come to pillage the fruits
that you hold out, on your unreachable crests,
to the people of the stars and the tribe of the winds,
nor to tear down the flowers I have never seen before,
meaning to wear them or hide some shame I overlook,
I who am a child of barren hills.

But it suddenly came to me in my last sleep
that always I was tethered in the lianas of the night
like the old pirogue of fables
in which all the days of my youth were passed,
from the shores of evening to the shores of dawn,
from the cape of the moon to the cape of the sun.

I've hauled myself out, and here at your heart I am,
    mountain of plants!
Here I have come to question your absolute silence,
to seek for the place where the winds are hatched
before they reach us, their wings full of holes,

broken by the immense net of the deserts
and by the snares of inhabited towns.

What do I hear and see, tallest of trees?
Here are lost sounds to recover which are lost again,
like underground rivers
crossed by enormous blind birds
carried off by the rapid currents
to be engulfed in slime.

It's your breath, your breath so deep
and already as sore as an old man's
climbing the coast of his memories
descending the slope of his exhausted days.
Your breath, and the breath of innumerable birds,
and of your branches grazed by the whole apocalyptic world.

But what may I see in your colourless night,
your night lasting longer than the death of virtuous men,
and the life of the wretched poor,
cave of leaves, out of which maybe
    one passage leads to the shore
and another to the horizon's hell,
you like a rainbow binding the continents?

I see nothing but the sun sinking,
like a pig assegaied in the scrub of the sky,
pig of light taken in powerful nets
that you spring in your ripe fruit and tough flowers,
high up, down there, at the extreme limit
where the spirit of earth and the force of the tree meet.

But later, even though the days are numberless
as your succession of leaves already fallen to hell,
even though the sevenfold nights have thickened

the night of time more than seven times,
so that I may gather the flowering dawns
at the end of the broken stalks of dusk,
I will always keep the memory of your silence
and of your strange clarity.

They'll be like pebbles thrown on the sand,
collected by an old sailor
who carries them home, placing them besides the shell
of a balanced miniature pirogue
bought in a distant isle that only a dream inhabits,
but where huts line the sea.

Rather they'll be like unworked pieces of ebony,
of rosewood or some other precious stuff
that I will place on my table
where your memory will slowly carve them
into fetishes with glassy eyes,
silent fetishes between my books.

(*Staffrider*, Volume 9, Number 3, 1991)

Zebu

Arched like the towns of Imerina
    clear on the rocky hills
    or cut from the very slopes;
    humped like the gables
    the moon sculpts on the soil,
    here is the powerful bull
    crimson as the colour of his blood.

He has drunk from the landings of rivers,
    grazed on cactuses and lilacs;
    here he crouches before manioc
    heavy still with the scent of the earth,
    and before the stems of rice
    that reek strongly of sun and shade.

Evening has dug down everywhere
    and the horizon is no more.
    The bull sees a desert that stretches
    right to the frontiers of the night.
    His horns are like a crescent
    moon rising.

Desert, desert,
    desert before the powerful bull
    who strays with the evening
    in the kingdom of silence,
    what do you recall in his half-sleep?
    Is it his kind without the hump,
    and are they red like the dust
    their passage raises,
    these, the masters of uninhabited lands?
    Or his sires the peasants fattened
    and led into towns, adorned with ripe oranges,
    to be felled in the King's honour?

He leaps, he bellows,
    he who will die without glory,
    then he sleeps again as he waits,
    resembles a hunch of soil.

(1934)

(*Staffrider*, Volume 11, Numbers 1–4, 1993)

Last Journal

At 9 minutes to 2 on my watch
I take 14 pills of 0.25 grams quinine
to muffle my head well.
A little water to swallow them.

At the age of Guerin, at the age of Deubel,
a little bit older than you, Rimbaud Next to Nothing,
because this life for us is too unsuitable
and because the bee has exhausted all pollen,
there is nothing left to argue and nothing left to wait for
and, laid down on the grit or the stone, deep in the grass,
    to gaze tenderly
on all those who one day like sheaves will be gathered.
Fixing a tender gaze! The tenderness of absence,
Next to Nothing, Nothing in which I can hardly believe.
    But is there a presence more pure
than may be rendered to you, O sweet Mother, O Earth?
We will all find ourselves in your solitude,
as peopled and as empty as the ocean.
And each time up here the wind of the south blows,
down there it will cause survivors.
What roots of flowers we will come to drink then
to calm in the sun such a thirst for the fruit.
Over us will bend the heliotropes of evening
and come to take from our secrets the Row.
This Row, the Noise of humans – the false rumours of shells
for sailors asleep in the slumber of the earth!
The Noise, the human Row, always the same in all ages
which only among the dead undresses some small part of your
    distress.
But already I sense the odour of dust
and of grass; already I hear the call of my girl;

ah! slowly forgotten her eyes hollow with earth,
of us she may dream in our tranquil caves!
And that which is not ready to shed tears
before our door closes in silence!
What may one think if there is no longer any charm,
some day, to be guided by us into that immense end …

At 2.37 on my watch.
The effect of the quinine is now felt.
Soon in a little sweetened water I shall take
more than 10 grams of potassium cyanide.

   – I stroke the family album. I send a kiss
to the works of Baudelaire which I have in the other room.
   – 15.02. I will drink – I have done. Mary, my children,
to you my thoughts – my last.

   I swallow a little sugar. I suffocate. I am going to stretch out.

(22 June, 1937)

Short-lived **Robert-Jules Allain** (1905–1934) was born of a French father and Malagasy mother. He became noted with Rabéarivelo as one of the founders of the spirited *Capricorne*, which he edited for six numbers from October, 1930. *Capricorne* was a monthly literary review of French-language and indigenous literature to which outsiders like Robert-Edward Hart of Mauritius contributed in order to establish a wider Indian Ocean school of writing. The following poem of Allain's is typical of those delicate, dreamy lyricists of the Southern ocean of the day.

Song of the South

My porters loaded with fruit
and my heart charged with dreams,
we return along the shore
of still waters soundlessly.

Under the fig-tree's heavy shade
and beneath the sun, we pass on,
I carried by them sweating,
they in the sphere of song.

And through the dale of the old mountain
we proceed, I balancing
in the azure filled with silence
on four nearly naked men.

(1931)

Jacques Rabémananjara (originally Jacques-Félicien) was born into a high-born family in 1913 in the province of Tamatave and educated in Antananarivo. In 1935 he was a founder of the *Revue des Jeunes de Madagascar*, which expressed an indigenous spirit. In Paris from 1939 he studied letters at the Sorbonne, associating with the black intellectuals launching the Negritude movement standing for the emancipation of the territories of the French Empire. Ready after the Second World War to fight for autonomy, they had particularly from 1947 as their mouthpiece the journal, *Présence Africaine*, with which Rabémananjara has long been associated and with whose press he has published his seven poetry collections. Notoriously in 1947 he was arrested with two other Madagascan deputies, on the suspicion of having been a party to the 1947 revolt, which led to a massacre and pacification by the French troops. He was sentenced to life with hard labour. During the following nine years he wrote several famous poems from prison, including "Complainte", which is reproduced below. Amnestied in 1956, he attended the First and Second Congresses of Black Writers, in 1957 taking the opportunity to celebrate there the thirtieth anniversary of Rabéarivelo's death by reading from his work, as well as Thomas Rahandraha's poem also included here. Returning to Madagascar in 1960, he became a minister of various departments including Foreign Affairs in the newly independent government of the first Malagasy Republic, and duly its Vice-president. By 1968 he was contributing the definitive description of his country and its culture to South Africa's *Optima* journal ("A Unified Madagascar Looks Ahead", published in December), though subsequently he was to become one of the leading figures to boycott South Africa on account of its apartheid policies. For example, in the 1986 special issue of *Présence Africaine,* devoted to 'South Africa Today', there is an account of a round-table discussion he chaired in Paris (with Miriam Tlali, Sipho Sepamla and Maishe Maponya) for the Société Africaine de Culture where the participants called for sanctions against the South African government. Long considered the successor of Rabéarivelo, at a colloquium held at the University of Madagascar in May, 1987, on the fiftieth anniversary of the latter's demise, Rabémananjara said of his friend of old: "This autodidact, who had the grand merit of having inscribed his name as the first Malgache one in the universal encyclopedia of poetry." In 1988 Rabémananjara was the third recipient, and the first from Africa, to be awarded the Grand Prix de la Francophonie by the French Academy. In an interview with Jean-Luc Raharimanana in the *Notre Librairie* issue of September, 1992, he stated that he no longer pushed the concept of 'Malgachitude', the spin-off of the Negritude philosophy, but had come round to supporting the school of 'malgachéité' – this suggests he came to practise a more internal exploration of his culture for home use rather than the assertive style of activism of previous decades, which he felt had been addressed to external readers. Rabémananjara has consistently stood for a unique Malagasy culture which, while being related to that of Africa at large, stands separately from it.

Lament

Blue, so blue that eye of the sky
    behind the window pane!
Life is in flower between my lashes,
Unbroken azure within my eyelids.
Blue, so blue that eye of the sky
    behind the window pane!

Dreary, so dreary these four walls!
Death imbues this earth and stone
with the damp of some other planet …
Lively, so lively those children's cries
    in the courtyard!

But who, bright innocence, will hear
    your song so pure,
    your voice too sweet,
in the uproar of the night?

The blind force of the abyss
    draws out with its lash
the shrill sound of agony!
The tender flesh of sorrow
bleeds at the kiss of the rope.

The stars die without a sigh.
What hand raised at the horizon
will tender to the lips of heroes
the red offering of dawn?

I have shed not one drop of blood,
I have sown no death at all,

my fingers are as clean as springtime,
my heart is as fresh as the Host.

But who, pure fighter, will ever hear
    your too innocent voice,
      your saddest of songs
in this croaking of darkness?

Blue, so blue that eye of the sky
    behind the iron bars,
Lively, so lively those children's cries
    on the lawn!

Life is in flower between my lashes,
unbroken azure within my eyelids,
innocence between the folds of my soul.

Civil Prison, Antananarivo,
12 June, 1947

The Seven-stringed Lyre

You were mine before you were made,
Mine even before the memory of the age-old gods.
Consecration is all mine!
My love is all the coronation and confirmation
    your splendour needs!
Uncountable centuries have gone by
Only to prefigure our messages,
To tune up our direct voice
And
Set loose the natural talent in our feet.

(*Contrast*, Cape Town, Number 28, April, 1972)

Flavien Ranaivo was born in 1914 in Arivonimano, where his father was governor of the district. He was educated at Gallieni School in the capital and his further studies qualified him as a prehistorian and archeologist of the Indian Ocean African region. He became an inspector of posts and telegraphs and subsequently a representative of his country at UNESCO. His first pamphlet of poetry was published in Antananarivo in 1947 with a preface by Octave Mannoni, the colonial psychologist who would become renowned for his *Prospero and Caliban*, which attempted to account for the 1947 rebellion. In 1955 Ranaivo published his second collection in Paris, with a preface by Senghor, who had already included five Ranaivo items in his 1948 anthology. An article of Ranaivo's on the burgeoning pre-independence literature of Madagascar was published in the magazine of the Mairies et Chambres Économiques d'Outre-Mer (in the Nouvelle Serie, Number 4 of October–December, 1969, edited in Martinique). At the time he was billed as the Director General of Information for Radio, Television and Traditional Arts in Antananarivo. This was published in an English translation by François Jacques in *Contrast*, Number 18 of April, 1972, and included literal translations of three poems by Rabéarivelo with some other examples used as illustrations, together with two of Ranaivo's own most famous poems, "Ne m'aimez pas" of 1947 and "Prémices" of 1962. The first of these had already appeared as "Love Song" in *Africa South* in a Koshland version, included below, and subsequently was taken up in *Black Orpheus*, Ibadan, in June, 1961, and then in *IZWI* in a much fuller translation into Afrikaans made in collaboration with Wilma Stockenström (with a preview published in *Rapport*); the second poem appeared attached to the article in *Contrast*. The former is a paraphrase and reworking of the traditional Madagascan 'hainteny', which Ranaivo describes as spontaneous poems which have become popular and which, as he pays tribute, began to be known in the West in printed form thanks to the collector Jean Paulhan, among others. According to Lilyan Kesteloot (in the *Anthologie Negro-Africaine* of 1967 and in later editions), Ranaivo became the real successor of Rabéarivelo for his complete break with continental poetic conventions, while exploring the potential of Malagasy material in newly stripped-down French. In 1979, in the *Modern Poetry in Translation* issue devoted to Francophone poetry of Africa, his "Love Song" (now called "Simple Lover's Song"!), was the only item to be included from the entire Indian Ocean region; and it has been reproduced numerous times since. In the anthology, *Voices from Madagascar* of 2002, another two of his poems appeared in excellent English versions made by one of the editors, Jacques Bourgeacq. He retired to live in France in 1973.

Love Song

Do not love me, my friend,
like your shadow –
shadows fade in the evening
and I will hold you
until the cock crows –
Do not love me like pepper,

it makes my belly too hot;
I cannot eat pepper
when I am hungry.
Do not love me like a pillow –
one would meet in sleep
and not see each other during the day.
Love me like a dream –
for dreams are your life in the night
and my hope in the day.

(Translated by Miriam Koshland, *Africa South*, Cape Town, Volume 4, Number 2, January – March, 1960)

Bemin my nie

Bemin my nie, my bloedverwante,
soos jou skaduwee,
want in die aand vervaag jou skaduwee
en vir jou wil ek hou
tot hanekraai;
nóg soos 'n rissie
wat my binnegoed verteer,
want dan sal ek nie
my honger kan versadig;
nóg soos 'n kopkussing,
want dan sal ons slapensure saam wees,
maar mekaar in the dag skaars sien;
nóg soos rys,
want sodra dit gesluk is, vergeet jy dit;
nóg soos vleitaal,
want dit verdamp;
nóg soos heuning,
lekker soet maar te doodgewoon.

Bemin my soos 'n lieflike droom,
jou lewe snags,
my hoop bedags;
soos 'n silwer muntstuk:
op aarde onafskeidbaar van my
en vir die groot reis
'n troue gesel;
soos 'n kalbas:
heel, 'n skepding vir water,
stukkend, bruggies vir my kitaar.

(Vertaal deur Wilma Stockenström en Stephen Gray, *Rapport*, 22 April, 1973, en *IZWI*, Nommer 16, 1 Junie, 1974)

First Fruits

Look at this poor water-lily,
living drowned in sorrow,
and dying with tears right up to its neck.
Like the man-with-the-silo-full-of-rice,
he is happy in the company of so many others
when he is greeted three times by the women passing by,
and even the most beautiful girl in town
promises him a strange and intimate love.

(*Contrast*, Cape Town, Number 28, April, 1972)

Regrets

Six paths
set out from the foot of the traveller's tree:
the first leads to the village-of-oblivion,
the second is a blind alley,
the third one is really not much good,
the fourth saw the best-loved pass by
but did not keep a spoor of her steps,
the fifth
is for whoever is gnawed with regret,
and the last ...
I'm not sure if it's passable.

(1955)

Carry Me Away

Carry me away,
carry me, O my very own feet,
at last to join that route again,
that route down there shaded by both
shifting leaves and leafy branches:
it's a long time that I haven't seen
my father and my mother.

(1962)

Dox is the pseudonym of Jean Verdi Salomon Razakandraina (1913–1978), a popular writer, musician and humorist, the first modern Madagascan to make a living entirely from his art. He was one of the founders of the post-war UPEM (Union des Poètes et Écrivains Malgaches), the organisation promoting both French-language literature and the local product, with its review, *Tatamo* (short-lived in the mid-1960s). The organisation still functions with its head office in Antananarivo, together with the Havatsa network, established to document and preserve the Malagasy language. Celebrated to this day for his independent minded expressions, his bearded, grisled portrait on a banner outside the capital's Municipal Library was the only one of half a dozen writers the students there were immediately able to identify. A commemorative collection of his poems in both languages, under the title *Chants Capricorniens,* was published by the Centre Culturel Albert Camus in Antananarivo in 1991. The 'ravinala' ('ravenale' in French) or fan-palm is chosen as the emblem of the Malagasy Republic, as in its folds it provides water to drink, the pulp may be eaten and the leaves provide shade against rain and sun.

Traveller's Tree

I've always had this thirst
which nothing assuages ...
And when I learned
that there is a certain water,
most refreshing of all,

that of the ravenales,
I went to look for
those trees.
I followed the path
through all the ferns,
I clambered under the bamboo
in arches
bound up with creepers
to arrive at
the impenetrable forest
of well-shaped, dense columns.
On the summit of a hill
I caught sight of
a whole row of ravenales!
What a disappointment! ... How ridiculous!
It is true
that their appeal is quite unique,
but how does one reach
up to their crowns?
At their base the first leaves
are all dried out.
They're pleasing to the eye
but only to flout it,
because these 'traveller's trees'
grow down the slippery sides
of damp ravines,
down inaccessible slopes!
And I cried out:
You ravenales, you mock my thirst!

Baobabs

You soar
colossal,
but still
you are delicate as a child:
Baobab ...
destitute,
a gigantic bottle
emptied of its water ...
Have your leaves been torn off,
from now on disappeared?
Your naked hands
hold up the spectre
of a rabble in agony
crying their litany to the skies ...
No shelter
for the tired voyager
who rests at your foot!
What prayers
do these naked hands
cast up?
It's so that the drought
should cease!
Poor thing!
Without even
flowers ...
living in empty space
damaged
worn away
by Nature
and disinherited
like Her.

Elie-Charles Abraham (1919–1989) was born in Tananarive, as it was then called, and followed the career of teacher and translator, editing several bilingual journals dedicated to the two Malagasy literatures, including the wonderful *Tatamo*. In Régis Rajemisa-Raolison's *Les Poétes Malgaches d'Expression Française* his work holds a central place. The poem included here appeared at about the same time in his last volume, *Pétales* (1986).

I Belong to Tana

Flowers. Light. Perfumes. Fiery looks everywhere.
Smiles as fresh as crystal water flows.
Everywhere the rhythm of jazz, the foxtrot and scherzos.
Airs of the tango, the waltz et cetera. In the soul stir
Memories. Numerous dreams. Numerous echoes.

The aroma of drinks. The cigarettes' haze.
The mysterious frou-frou of satin dresses.
The slow murmurs of love the morning surprises.
Sighs. The noisy laugh. Caresses. Flirts. Words of praise.
Amazed couples snap their fingers at fate's disguises.

Tonight quite simply Tana amuses itself.
The City of a Thousand with its absent hours.
It's a ball in the woods – in a square of flowers.
All is light, joy, harmony. O my Muse herself!
The whole Town dances and smiling Love towers!

I'm attached to Tana, to its elegant soirées.
I share its torchlight, its cries, its song.
And the Theatre, the Cinemas – I write as I belong.

Why not after all, Town of my youthful days?
Would I be ashamed, Tana, to be your son?

Tana, Square Poincaré, Saturday 6 May, 1945

The capital named Antananarivo or the Citadel of a Thousand Warriors – Tana for short – had been invaded by Springbok troops three years previously to unseat its Vichy government. This poem was written two days before the unconditional surrender of the Nazi regime in Europe and hence the victory of De Gaulle's troops in France, the motherland.

Esther Nirina is the pen-name of Esther Rabémananjara (no relation) (1932–2004) who, after many years as a librarian in France, returned to her home country of Madagascar in 1990. Her four poetry pamphlets, which received high honour, were collected together with new poems in a substantial volume in 1998: *Rien que Lune*, published by Éditions Grand Océan, with a preface by Édouard J. Maunick.

Prose Poem

Sweet and soft morning light. A rosy gold mist bathes the atmosphere. A winter Sunday morning.

A bird launches its call from the top of the rose-bush: another bird inspects the fig-tree in the garden. A call? Rather a recall of the celebration expected in advance. A choice complicity.

The day is about to begin.
　I am the breath of the flowering park.
　Everything seems alive, busy with the verb 'to love'.
　My hands perform the most simple movements naturally: drawing the curtains to find a place for the sun's vibrations, its oblique rays unconsciously touching the floorboards, the furniture and various objects. Sun more and more confident, extending right to the roots of the heart. To be at the same time spirit and matter: tying the flowers into a bouquet of prayer. Circulating from one room to the next, but calmly none the less, cheerful!

Laying the table in a solemn, sober fashion, choosing the plates on which the dishes to be shared will be placed. Checking with a peek the boiling rice. Elementary acts, but privileged ones which calm one:

here's natural water ... Help yourself to bread. A festive atmosphere. Festive air without fussing.

The hour is no more than an instant away
    Now will be the moment
    Attentive ... for the least sign of his arrival
    Waiting: prelude to the celebration
    Waiting anxiously precedes the delay.

Delay at last defines that his absence has become real. Like a smile withheld.

Time stays still.
    An indefinite stop
    Hope wastes away bit by bit.

Another threshold has been crossed. A narrow porch through which I learnt to see the dawn of childhood, when I grew older. To learn how to live the illusion, to be able to embrace the frozen image, O how inevitable, of death which ends by giving life.
    The stillness of time weighs heavily on me. I myself feel as though I am a single word in a book.

Thomas Rahandraha has been known as a science professor at the university in Antananarivo. His "Appeal", previously entitled "The Poet", first appeared quoted in Jacques Rabémananjara's "Le Poète Noir et Son Peuple" in *Présence Africaine* in October–November, 1957, and was later included in the 'New Sum of Poetry from the Negro World' issue of *Présence Africaine* (Number 57 of January–March, 1966), together with two poems by Lucien Xavier Michel Andrianarahinjaka, as well as early work by Édouard Maunick, those three representing the Indian Ocean African islands there. By December, 1966, an early English version had appeared in *The New African*, London, translated by Willfried Feuser. "Appeal" has been frequently reprinted in anthologies devoted to Negritude and, as a precursor, it is a key item in Liliane Ramarosoa's *Anthologie de la Littérature Malgache d'Expression Française des Années 80*. The first translation into English available to South Africans was made by Dorothy Blair and was included in her article published in *Contrast* (in Number 3 of Winter, 1961).

Appeal

> You whom the gods have elected
> so that our springs should run with song
>   and our forests ring with sap,
> so that, arid or grassy
>   our mountains stay mountains
> so that earth stays the earth
>   fervour our breath

    faithful our hearts
    and all our men be men

from the greatest depth of your soul
from the tumult of your blood
from the light of our dreams
from the most stormy of your desires
from the most intense of your incantations
    ah, may the power of your belief burst forth
    the cry of their deliverance
        you will speak
you will speak the language of your purity
for those whose voice is walled in
and life suspended

you will speak the language of your innocence
for those who are crushed with calumny
until their very skin sweats it out
you will speak the language of your justice
for those who have their view blinded
by the iron of the prison bars

you will speak of your love
for those who are beaten
for those who are stifled
for those who are tortured
for those trapped
            you will speak
for those condemned
            you will speak
for those deported
            you will speak
for those awaiting trial
            you will speak
for the detainees

                        you will speak
for the indicted
                        you will speak
for the defenceless
                        you will speak

for the thousands of people dead among the dead
    who are destined to the fury and the hatred
        in the darkness of prison
            you will speak

        because you hate violence
            you hate calumny
            you hate untruth
            you hate hatred
                you'll speak

        to them too, you will speak

you will speak to the ends of the sea and of the night
    so that the day may dawn
    and for them once again
    our springs run with song
    and our forests ring with sap
    so that, arid or grassy,
    our mountains stay mountains
    so that earth is earth
    fervour our breath
    faithful our hearts
    and allow men to be men
your being is the word reconciled in life
                speak …

Henri Rahaingoson was born in Antananarivo in 1938 and is distinguished as a translator and educator. Currently he is the president of Havatsa-UPEM, one of the country's organisations for writers in French and for the promotion of the Malagasy language and its culture. His self-produced collection of poems goes by the title *Poèmes Inné-Di* …, playing on the fact that they are as yet unpublished and by one 'Di' (his pseudonym); half the contents is written in French, dating back to the 1960s, and the rest is his own translations from French into Malagasy.

The Attractions of Oblivion
(To Jean-Joseph Rabéarivelo)

All time shed, J.-J.,
Child of the dark border,
All time shed and then withered,
The refrains of yesterday and our songs of that time …
And the drunken heart

And my heart drunk on having read your books,
O sombre child of unknown shores,
No longer to be recovered …

Tell me, J.-J., yes tell,
Tell me what there is down there:
Nothingness? A Paradise?
Were those the Sirens who guided your steps?
And your thirst and your quest

After those famous nectars and liquors of forgetfulness,
Did they satisfy?

Or rather, quite simply,
Answer: O dark child:
About shores, about down there, the country of nowhere,
Tomorrow ...
Or right now!
What the hell, give me your hand!
Because ...
A desire grips me as well
... To untie the ropes.

(1960)

For a Departure

For better or for the worse
And on the boat of destiny
One fine morning you went free:
I sigh for this rueful verse.

On that dawn at the Old Port
echoing the grand farewell
you left, but somewhere else
a friend of before cries on distraught.

He remembers there was a time of plenty
bursting with promises and dreams,
strewn with laughter and joy, it seems,
when you and he were not yet twenty.

But so one day, I'm not sure when,
Another arrived, only by chance,
Cradling you in his romance,
And you, well – you just pissed off then.

And now on this steamer by slow degrees
Out on the bridge, hand in hand,
Sailing out to another land,
You're taking off for open seas

While your true friend stays on the quay
Having eyed so long and ever
The blue route of every lover –
But you haven't even noticed me.

(1963)

Cacomania

Lullaby me, O Cacomania,
In the counter-rhythms of barbaric music
So that bang! crash!
I will deconform myself
From this shameful decency of old nuns
Whose never-ending theme is of
Comedy Baby Jesuses,
Of 'behave correctly',
Because I'm right up to here
With touching up choirboys like this,
In their eternal, artificial begging song.

Compel me, O Hater of Falsehood,

To fall in love
With a clown –
But a real one
Who breathes circus right into his entrails;
Yes, a clown close-up
Who caricatures
The furtive sneer of vices badly camouflaged,
Revealing sometimes
The horizon of a glance
And the frontier of a lip.

Because I wish to learn
How one may anarchise
That false melody
Of this paperpushing, red-taped existence,
So that by brick! by broke!
I may chant out and cry with all my soul
The hymn of the rubbish bins
The measure and echo
– A choir without words –
Of those fat blue flies.

Oh, let me sing out the splendour of stenches,
Live in the drunkenness
Of speckles of dirty ribaldry,
To spit out the bad temper and dislike
Of those decorated with such orders
And the rewards of virtue!

They'll inform me, of course, that I am not right in the head,
I'm an antisocial fool, or just plain dumb!
What does it matter? And I'll reply,
For at least what's unseemly is true:
"Whatever's true is utterly beautiful!"

So now, that I prefer to all your false show.

(1963)

Written as an enraged schoolboy, taught in colonial schools to imitate France but never to become truly French. Empire citizens should rather achieve the status of 'Francophonie' (which rimes with 'cacophony'). The secondary meaning of 'caco-' will be obvious to all South Africans.

Serge Henri Rodin was born in 1949 and teaches literature at Antananarivo's university, where he acts as the Madagascan representative of the Grand Océan poetry publishing initiative, based in Réunion. He also represented his country at the Inter-regional Poetry Festival of 2003, held in Réunion, where he presented these poems.

Dog Sun

In a hostile, real universe,
very real and authentic, the last
predators, an episode of the chaotic
life of a fugitive of the City,
mixed into the rabble.

Untitled

The sweat of the paving-stones
reflects the sky poorly
and the holes in those stones
make reality lament

the red earth of the fathers
rises across their pores,
the reddened grass of the paving
makes me believe again in dawn

polished, grey and smooth,
the heavy cobbles of our streets.

The anthropologist, **Élie Rajaonarison**, was born in Ambatondrazaka (in 1951) and is considered by many the leader of the next generation of writers after Rabémananjara and Ranaivo. His collection of poems, *Ranitra*, was published in 1992. The prose piece of his, translated into English in *Revue Noire* (Number 16 of September – November, 1997) as "Wake Up! We are All Dead!", is characteristic of his cultural activism and includes the poem excerpted here. Since 1982 he has been the president-founder of the Sandratra writers' circle, which specialises in touring Madagascar to give public readings and classes in writing.

Wake Up! We are All Dead!

A society has exactly the Art it deserves!
Between sky and sea, there's a cry rising in the desert:
Let's wake up! We're all of us dead ...
The mists sough with paralysed, stiff smiles
Over the standing stones

Wake up now! We're all the dead ...
But the deaf-mute witnesses of our unobliterated past
Are proudly rising

Let's wake up! We're all the dead ...
Will there be a glimmer still
In all this vanishing splendour?

Let's wake up!
The Beauty-to-be-Desired is dancing there

The Beloved-One-Longed-For smiles at her
Their children sing their heartbreaking song

Let's wake up!
The moon of Alakarabo is full
It causes the standing stones to shine
And the deaf-mutes to hum

Wake up!
Wake up!
The harvest will be good!

Message from My Children
(To the fire-raisers of the Land of the Ancestors)

They're burning it
all of it
the remains of the forest
which perfumed the air
they're burning the lot

the eyes with smarting
endure the smoke,
a landscape blackening
the stinking horizon

Man devoid of shame,
get yourself here!
Why do you hide
in this grotesqueness of night
to serve your needs,
why do you continue so,

for us to be prisoners
of a future desert?

Come over here to witness
all these birds
crying out for their habitat

Come here to listen to
such cries of the animals,
the earth's death-rattle

Come here to drink
the tears of the trees
cleared of the sky

Come right here
also to see struck
the acidity of the world:
bitter-black-emaciated.

Then you will think about it,
cease this burning riot –
find the peace to inhale
just one flower in bloom.

You sons of the night,
is it the eternal stubbornness
of your eternal manliness?
Agree to look

agree to savour
agree to meditate
and so to change.
But if you stumble one more time,
"You will be damned,

you and your descendants,
for all eternity."

Written on the RN4 at the Forestry Reserve of Manankazo, September, 1990

David Jaomanoro was born in the far north of Madagascar in 1953, where he has taught French in schools and been the director of cultural services of the region, specialising in Sakalava society. His short fiction has been honoured at various Francophone festivals. At present he is resident in Mayotte, where he contributes to the local literary review, *Le Bavard* (see Number 5 of September, 2004).

Anything Special This Morning?

Under a veranda
a child has died, died of hunger

Piled in, the one on the other
like the offspring of beasts
in their poverty they sprawl

During the night he was extinguished
quietly quietly
making a present to his pals
of his beggar's cap

One morning like all the rest
a street-child sleeps on forever
his mates observe him foolishly
without a word without a sob

But what is there special this morning?
Under a veranda
a child is dead, died of hunger.

Dina

    Dina
    daughter of the dawn
    fruit of hope
    my girl
you weep whenever I sneeze
a bit too loudly
but when I chide you you smile
will you know
when I can no longer
make you dance on my chest
how to say
like the others – but so few –
he was really somebody?

    Dina
    I coo in your ear oh my best beloved
    Dina my love
will you know
when I can no longer
drink the gleaming and burning
laughter of your shady eyes
once with you I've become
breathless under tables and chairs
in the pursuit of happiness
how to read in turn
among the thousand kisses squeezed into this poem
the one I intended for you?

    Dina
    compact of blood
    my blood
I've sworn a vow

never to hate
as I have been hated betrayed
I have promised, Dina
that a flourishing star
a starry flower
picked in the prairie of tomorrow
will sparkle in the night of your hair
will you know
when I can no longer
read your face against the thatch blackened with soot
steal kisses from your sleep of an angel
suffer with happiness
as I hear your purest chattering
that I have given myself without complaint
nor with any regret entirely
to you?

Vololona Picard is Madagascan-born, but lives in Réunion. A substantial selection of her poetry was published there in 1998, under the title *De Jaspe et de Sang*, in the Collection La Roche écrite, by Éditions Grand Océan.

Eve Reading

Eve is reading
Parny's *Chansons Madécasses*
She turns towards me
Tell me
How much do you love me?
I kneel
On the ground
Place my hand on my heart

Children not Listening

The children don't listen

Their glances
Light
As the breath
That stirs sometimes
The malarial breeze
Of the December solstice

Rushing from cobweb to cobweb
Where flies struggle
In their swaddling of silk

Whoever finds
The best spiderweb
With the most flies
Wins

Veromanitra Razafiarivony was born in 1965 in Antananarivo and became a student of Serge Henri Rodin. She is an active member of Sandratra, has broadcast poems on Radio Tana and participates in the literary events of the Centre Culturel Albert Camus there. She has not as yet had a poetry collection published.

Madagascar

My island, Madagascar,
Surrounded by a thousand isles.
My island is just like yours.
An isle isolated in the middle of the ocean.
If the ocean did not exist there
My isle would never have been known.
Sister islands, Overseas islands,
United by the Great Blue.

A Book

On the book of the Indian Ocean
The immense blue cover
Transports us off to paradise,
This blue colour alleviates all stupid fears
Which make our souls tremble.
That is the warmth which burns up our patience.
But the reading continues:

Within a few pages
The whales honour this ocean,
Their annual migration a privilege,
Proud they are of their dance
Sharing the oceanic pleasure,
Their flexible bodies bending
Beneath the surface of the sea.

A Poem Reflecting My Life

When I take the decision
Not to follow you into that far country
With its wealthy sweet ways,
I still love you more than my life,
But I'm afraid of being cut off
In such a spectacular world.
That valley of silver would prevent me
From visiting Rasoanilaina whom I need so much,
She who dresses my hair in Merina tresses,
So easy to do and which honour me
Like a lady with a newborn child.

And now, so our parting begins.
You leave for gain and I leave for life,
Your courtesy is not enough to live Malgache-style:
I grind the rice; I plant the paddy;
With pistachio I cook the cassava.
I die losing you. You're off to your fate,
To plant yourself anew on the soil of sweat,
Foreign soil where I'd never find
My own sense of belonging,
My negress skin, my frizzy hair,
My beauty would wither away in that land of riches.

Jean-Luc Raharimanana, born in 1967 in Antananarivo, is a journalist and teacher. In 1987 one of his poems won the competition held to mark the fiftieth anniversary of Rabéarivelo's death. Since leaving Madagascar on a study bursary in 1989 for Paris he has developed an international reputation, with three works of fiction published by Le Serpent à Plumes, and he holds a prominent place in *Voices from Madagascar: An Anthology of Contemporary Francophone Literature*, edited with originals and translations by Jacques Bourgeacq and Liliane Ramarosoa (published by the Ohio University Center for International Studies, Athens, Ohio, in 2002). He is much travelled as a representative of his country. In 2004 he returned to his home to produce his scathing report on conditions in *L'Arbre Anthropophages*. The following two poems are from an as yet unpublished collection.

The Habit of Writing

The habit of writing, once acquired
    prevents the spirit from wandering
It endeavours to throw you into the midst
    of a circle of words
Words which ceaselessly come back to
    pester you
King-words: Destiny, Love, Joy
    Sadness
Prince-words: Sun, Moon, Blue
    Dusk
Slave-words: teardrops, despair
    blood and sweat, words that serve

the thirst for life.
You take out the blank page
Kiss of ink
For a poem-child.

Ecstatic.

A Crematory Poem

It's peaceful when the dust is on alert
Beneath the boot of the soldier
Peaceful when the street-child
Coils against the silent doors
Peaceful when at the convent threshold
Abandoned babies wail
Peaceful when in the comfy sewers
The bodies of those one believed alive
Stink.
A peace that kills you!
The word that violates my mouth tastes good.
I say: Kill, *kill!*

Ndrivo is the pseudonym of Andriamboavonjy Andrianarivo, one of the group of younger poets of the region who practise the fresh style of assertive oral delivery, derived from rap and other African-American influences – in short, the next in line after Negritude, Malgachitude, Oceanitude and Coolitude: Slamitude. He participates in the monthly open sessions held at the Albert Camus Cultural Centre in Antananarivo.

Tattoo Art

I'm a painter on living flesh
I practise tattoos as art
I paint without a brush
I tattoo with all my heart

It's epidermal, no need to strike
To engrave beneath the skin
Rather than on a stony rock
I'm a painter on living flesh

I design there or where you wish
I haunt each anatomical part
I scrawl whatever you relish
I practise tattoo art

No need of any liquid wash
I am no watercolourist
I'm a sado-piercing specialist
I paint without a brush

Occasionally for lovely eyes
I deploy each coloured dart
And after I prick blood and the bruises
I tattoo with all my heart

I'm a painter on broken flesh
I'm an artist of radiant light
I don't paint only for the cash
When I tattoo in black and white

No passport needed where I'm god
I've a licence to tattoo every
Member of all humanity
I'm a painter on your body

Between graffiti in blood red
I've not yet finished my story
With characters in scenes of love instead
I am an artist of the living core

With me each border's dot and dash
Some take me for their gynaeco
To autograph their 'little prow'
I don't paint only for the cash

But my masterpiece is still on track
On parchment hide in time's despite
I decipher the long days' slow defile
When I tattoo in black and white

I am a painter on living flesh
I practise tattoos as art
I insinuate without a brush
I pierce with all my heart

Tombo is the stage-name of **Tomboarivo Ravalihasy**, born in Antananarivo in 1980. He is an organiser of the city's slam movement and chairs regular sessions. His poem here, "Frimousse", translated line for line, has all but six lines beginning with 'Fr-', with many internal alliterations on the same consonants.

Pretty Face

Pretty Face,
all fake and
frippery.
Want to flourish a while?
So fresh you are.
The friction of
your rustling frock,
the freshness of your
coldly fragrant perfume to me
seems frivolous!

Felled by the affront of the enemy sex,
I fraternise and make pacts, yet only receive
the frown of your brow
and a frozen look
on your part, instead of a
phrase of welcome!

To listen to you
humming the
frigid refrain of the chastity belt of your spiky
defence, the impassable
frontier so fixèd,

closed to the confrontation of a feverish heart's
beating out a path to you.

Then falls on me the
foul and horrid truth of the frightful evidence! Sad picture!
Your frangipani will flower only on the stench of the usufruct,
you'll mess with a
filthy rich
playboy flirt,
who offers you just fripperies:
a false verdict, I am condemned to frustration.

Crumple up one so felonious,
a scoundrel, one who's trifling
small fry. I finish by
curbing my fervour and crying my
assassin's phrase:

"Fake, Pretty Face!
Show off, but why not
shiver a bit too? For:
forbidden fruit you may well be, but frankly
putrid fruit's your future day!"

Lazawell is the nickname of Andry Solofo Andriamiariseta, born in Antananarivo in 1975. Although he has not yet published a collection of poems, he has made radio broadcasts of his work and to keep alive works as the manager of a shirt factory. He is researching the life and work of Rabéarivelo, with a view to publishing on the seventieth anniversary of his death (in 2007). The original title of his poem is in English, being a reference to Bob Marley.

"Get Up! Stand Up!"

Today
is
a great day.
A truce.
A rest of
meditation.
A new departure.
Wild-eyed.
Eternity.
A fiction.

A wake-up call
to the sweet life,
a creature in movement,
a bottling up of caresses,
stage by stage,
preliminary,
seductive,
face to face, a transport
to a well-fed rest.

Today
is
a great day.
A truce.
A meditation rest.
An eternity of fiction.

(2006)

SEYCHELLES

The Nanny Who Wanted to Marry (traditional)

An old nanny had charge of a little English girl. One day she found a large louse in her charge's hair. It was indeed a big louse, as big as that – if not: bigger. It was so big that she took it to her home with her, skinned it and stretched its skin over a drum. Then the nanny went out and around the town, beating her new drum.

To every man she met she said: "If you guess what my drum is made of I'll marry you."

But no one could guess right.

"A pig's skin," said one.

"A goat's skin," said another.

"A calf's skin," said a third.

Still beating her drum, she went down to the end of the long pier. In the turtle pool was an old turtle from Aldabra. He was swimming about and sighing for all his companions, who had been taken out and eaten one by one. And he was weeping because it was his turn next.

"Turtle," said the old woman, "I have told my charge never to eat turtle soup. If you guess what my drum is made of, I'll marry you."

"A turtle's stomach, I suppose," he said with a deep sigh.

"No."

"No? Then for all I care it may be the skin of a louse."

"Good," said the old woman, "and for that I'll take you home and marry you."

So she had him hauled out of the pond by one flipper and loaded, still sighing dreadfully, on to a cart. By the time they got him home, it was late, so she had him laid on his back outside the house.

"Stay there," she told him, "and in the morning I'll marry you." And she left him there for the night, sighing and shedding tears for his companions.

But when she came out early in the morning she found, to her surprise, only his empty shell lying where she had left it. But beside it stood a beautiful smiling boy.

This she rushed to tell the little English girl.

(Collected by F. D. Ommanney in *The Shoals of Capricorn*, London: Longmans, Green, 1952)

Antoine Abel was born in 1934 on Mahé, the main island of the Seychelles. He went to school there and studied further at the Universities of Reading and of Bristol, returning to teach in Victoria, the capital. He has written short stories and collected oral pieces for publication. His first poetry volume appeared in 1969. The poems below are from his collection *Contes et Poèmes des Seychelles*, published in Paris in 1977.

Your Country

Your country
Is studded with mountains,
Seychelles lad.

With tough granite
With crude gravel
And with coral, your country.

Your country
Wears a belt
Of white beaches loosening in the tides.

What You are

A mixture of blood
Coupled with a vegetal scramble ...
Race or people or nation?
Claim whatever you want;

Interpret his skin
And you'll see
A mixture,
A fish-trap,
A cosmos.
Huts,
Cabins,
Colonial roofs.
He speaks
The language,
The tongue,
The expression,
The phonetic warmth,
A unique and varied universe,
A hybrid of sounds and colours.
A rainbow over the sky,
A dance of suns,
And the temperatures change carnally,
Physically, psychically …
An armful,
A spread of sail,
An elbow-length
Of negritude lost and recovered once more
On the threshold of the twenty-first century.

The Old Lady

She was returning from church.
It was eight o'clock in the morning.
She wore a black skirt, pleated,
A white coat with long sleeves
With the lace just about covering her hands.

She was armed with an umbrella
Which she never forgets.
On her head a linen doek
Knotted behind her neck,
With a little triangle to be seen
Behind each ear.
On top of all this a hat
Of raffia, ebony-coloured,
Crowning her venerable head,
And in her left hand an enormous fan,
A souvenir of her faded youth ...
And whenever she stops
At the top of the hill
She opens it like a young girl ...
Dahlia makes no delay.
And with one agile step like a moorhen
She strides down the side of the hill
On the footpath that must lead to her house.
Her village? A hamlet
Amounting to three boats.

A Bat

I'm not a 'bald mouse' –
I don't know why the French call me that.
But nobody knows my bad temper.
They call me a night-bird.
The seagulls – symbol of hypocrisy –
Don't like to catch sight of me.
Mother Nature gave me these colours.
I refuse to change them.
Towards whichever locality where fruit
Is to be found I send my broadcasts

And my aerials capture the response.
When I set off I know precisely
Where I am to find my nourishment.
On the other hand I strongly fear
Human beings. They have firearms …
The other day a barricade of hail struck.
Rospatine and me – we tried to
Take refuge in a mango-tree. Alas!
Not a chance. My girlfriend was picked off
Even before I had time to tack.

Forgotten Land

You came back to the country of your forefathers
A suitcase in hand
First you went to visit the family house
What did you see?
This world has changed
The house was empty.

You climbed up to the cemetery
A wreath in hand
You searched among the graves
What did you see?
The earth is washed away
The tombs have disappeared.

Then you threw your wreath
Into the undergrowth
A tiny canary went to check
What was going on
It didn't touch the flowers
It flew off pretty quickly.

You took the first flight
Out of the country ...
Your visit was a disappointment
You felt forgotten in your home land.

COMOROS

Aboubacar Saïd Salim, who often writes under the pseudonym 'Abou', was born in 1949 in Moroni, nowadays the capital city of the Republic of the Comoros. He was educated in the Comoros and completed in France, teaching French in schools back home until in 1985 he was imprisoned for anti-mercenary sentiments. Since then he has held several prestigious government posts and is the founder of the Association des Poètes et Écrivains Comoriens. A short story of his, "The Revolt of the Vowels", translated into English by Carole Beckett, appeared in *The Picador Book of African Stories* in 2000. As a topical poet he contributes to *Kashkazi*, the newspaper edited in Moroni which advocates the reunification of the Comorian islands. The first poem here was written for the occasion of the inter-island poetry festival, Espaces de Paroles, held in Réunion in 2003.

Salaam Réunion, Salaam

Peace be with you, Bourbon Island,
Rich in history. A reunion
Of people, of cultures, of religions,
A hybrid of balances, woven through the centuries
Into a brilliant creole rainbow,

Of many and different celebrities, birthplace of
Leconte de Lisle the poet abolitionist,
Lhermitte the slave-captain, La Buse the pirate,
They have made your history riotous and rich.

And what to say of your soaring beauty, Réunion?

Bernica like a divine wound
Dressed in luxuriant nature
La Roche Écrite, Mafate, Plaine des Cafres,
Maïdo, Piton des Neiges, roof of the Indian Ocean
And the Fournaise, spitting the sacred fire of earth's innards.

Réunion, I bring you fraternal greetings
From your brothers of Karthala, of Ntingui and Tratringa,
Those of wise Trambwe the sultan of poetry
And not to forget those of the moon, queen
Of the perfumed isles of nature untouched.

But how I would also like to recall
The sad links with my country,
The memory of those transported for life
From one shore to another of our landfalls
And further, from one penal colony to another
From Mayotte to Cayenne
Shackles of suffering
Calling forth the brotherhood
Of our people dominated of old
By the same master.

Moroni my Sorrow

Capital city of my stricken country
Moroni, I pity your magnificent dusks
And the splendid dawns over the unspeakable
Poverty of your children, battered from coups d'état
To dictator's felony.

Moroni, city of fire!
You attempt desperately to inhale freely

But your incandescent breath
Mixes in with the sulphurous odours of Karthala
That volcano of a thousand tricks which awaits,
Tireless watchman, the least sign of freedom
Soon to strangle
With its magma of fire.

Moroni my sorrow, futility of paltry wealth,
In your noisy markets life is suspended
From ropes of the starving revenue
Of the unemployed, workers without work,
Civil servants who serve badly
At the theoretical end of the month.

Moroni my suffering, I grieve for your young
Brimming with life dreaming only of their
Departure visa
Like the castaway on his plank
Deluded by phantom eldorados
And so having to survive.

Moroni, city of a thousand mosques,
Your muezzins shout themselves wonderfully hoarse
God seems deaf to their prayers
Because for all their prostrations
Your idle offspring look like
Adoring only power, gold and silver.

Moroni, my city, clothed in arrogance and pride,
Moroni – 4 x 4
Moroni – Méganes
Moroni – Villas
Moroni – Palaces
Moroni – Croesus

Moroni – Indifference
Moroni – Straw hats
Moroni – Shantytown
Moroni – Stevedore
Moroni – Drudges
Moroni – Unemployed
Moroni – Filth

Moroni, rope-dancing town
Your chaotic life
Hangs on a thread
That of being aware
That you belong to the same soil
As all the other towns,
Even if, of the Lunar Isles,
You remain the lunatic capital!

(2003)

Mahamoud M'Saidie was born at M'dé, Bambao, in the Comoros in 1966 and has achieved his doctorate in France where he teaches. With L'Harmattan in 2001, he published a volume of poems, *Le Mur du Calvaire*, from which these two poems are taken.

The Sign of Water

Lady, they've asked me for my real name
Of birth.
Tell them that my backbone is brown,
Well cured with salt.
Tell them I have the keys to all the doors
Of the lagoons, that the odour of my guts
Is that of coral perfumed by the deep.

Lady, tell them that my body bears
Watery scales and my eyeball has taken on
The colour of rushes of lava.
Lady, lady, tell them that the sadness of water
Is inscribed in the drift of my veins.

Interview

Yesterday the mortuary dust was unloaded on
The tired out soul of the Seaweed-of-blood.
She nibbled at a few morsels of life.
And the wind across his balcony stood to one side,
Smiling at the disaster.

But a really ripe sun has gone to talk to him
Of the secrets of men:
Tells him to leave the Comorians alone.

Saïndoune Ben Ali was born facing the sea at Mirontsy on Anjouan at the end of the 1960s. His single, very influential volume of Comorian French-language poems, *Testaments de Transhumance*, from which all the poems below are selected, was published by Éditions Grand Océan in 1996, at which time he liked to announce that he had been trampled to death in 1978 by a carnivalesque reactionary crowd rioting with joy at the mercenaries' coup d'état against the socialist president, Ali Soilihi. A new edition of *Testaments* was published by KomÉdit in Moroni in 2004, with the same deceptive biography. Abdou Baco on Mayotte assured this editor with a twinkle that he should pursue collecting Ali's work, and on Madagascar Adjmaël Halidi informed him that Ali was indeed alive enough for Halidi to dedicate his life's work to him and was apparently happily devoting the rest of his days "to intoxication and debauchery". An article in *Africultures* by his friend Soeuf Elbadawi (Number 51 of October, 2002) explains all.

On the Beach

On the bare sand washed
by the last fertile waves
of this people,
would you be able to understand
perhaps the anxiety of a mother
filled with loneliness?

Like wings which have need of
wind, their children have left.

Getting Round

When I get round to counting
how many children bore
into the beds of sand in quest
of shell-fish at low tide
how many crows die
of hunger on the beach facing
the closed doors of the Kingdom-
of-Forbidden-Shadows
how many prayers become empty
of all meaning on the slopes
like mice of affliction

then I get round to permitting the President
to pass by without shaking his hand.

The Whores of Mutsamudu

The whores of Mutsamudu
measure us up from their balconies
thousands of years old like the stayover
houses of Yemen

between walls corroded with the ages
they deal cheerfully with an old townsman
who misses the nocturnal massages
of his grand-daughters

the whores of Mutsamudu
introduce us into their labyrinths
like she-devils preparing an orgy

down these corridors breeding up wasps
and the caymans of the old nobility
– I am the bastard who delivers you

Down There

Down there on the shingle, the old mothers sacrifice
clean white cocks in the fragrance of their madness
for the small gods of the ocean; a coralline monster
at the maw of a deep blue morgue calls out the alphabet
of our vanished ones in the drop by drop of our visions.
The martyrologists with their little starred flags
do not hide their constraint – do the drowned have a God?
And their faith in the Nation! this nation governed
by their meanness, old apes, fat leeches, big-bellied.
This nation where the surgeon complains of his appendicitis
or the high school lad exposes one day beneath a brick-red sun
his private parts to correct his mother, reading patriotic chants.
The inhabitant of these Moon islands
    travels through his summer sleep
as if cut off from his body, the lagoon and milky
putrefaction, a fly-trap, the sport of the ministers.

The Four Winds

Don't be a character
of Ben Okri's who must traverse
Stars of the New Curfew
don't be a character of Sartre's
never able to vomit out his world

be Romeo in a Congolese theatre
or that bird-man of Rushdie
who wants to cross the walls of
the blind gaze, but not Don Quixote
or Pantagruel, to win me back ...

nor Christophe of the eternal tragedies
or Shaka of glories of blood
or a Soilihi supporter of childish melancholy ...

the four winds in the sails of Adonis
space-man with the winds in hand

The socialist Ali Soilihi led a coup d'état one month after the Comoros became independent in 1975. He in turn was overthrown in 1978 and assassinated two months later by mercenaries with suspected South African connections.

Salim Hatubou was born in 1972 in the Comoros and grew up in La Solidarité, the northern quarter of Marseilles where many of the Comorian exiled community are based. He is the author of several books published since 1994 by L'Harmattan in Paris and by KomÉdit back in Moroni. The following text is from his *Métro Bougainville* of 2000, a collection of oral texts about the diaspora experience.

And So

So, with naked feet, I took to the path leading to the town. I went through the villages where I saw all the same poverty. I closed my eyes and I quickened my steps. I reached the pass. I arrived in town, out of breath and sweating. I said: I want to leave! The man looked at me, smiling. He asked me: Have you a strong back and tough arms? I answered: I'm as solid as the sacred rock of my village, as strong as the baobab of djinns of my forebears and as loyal as the fisherfolk's sons. He asked me: Name? I have the name of my father. Date of birth? I was born in the middle of the year of the great drought. Look down there, in the harbour, do you see the seagulls? Tomorrow, at dawn, you will make your way through there and board that ship.

Kamaroudine Abdallah Paune, originally Anjouanais, has long been resident in Mayotte where he has taught English in several schools. He has published two pamphlets of poetry in France in the Collection Sajat (2001 and 2002), in which he notes the obstacles Comorian poets normally face in attempting to get their work published.

Voyage

I'll take a trip over the horizon
To find whatever is hidden beyond
Those oceans and mysterious seas
Sending us ships
Filled with marvellous dreams.

I'll travel over the horizon
My island slung across my back,
And walk over there aimlessly
Among legends and visions,
So that I don't lose one drop
Of the rain of the stars,
Which fertilises earth
With the perpetual enchantment
Of sights and hearts.

I'll voyage over the ocean
To gather up the beauty and the bounty,
And plant them on my island,
So that they bring forth
The fruit of whatever we'll sow,
On all the isles of fear,

Of anxiety and of panic,
With peals of thunder.

I'll journey beyond it all
And bring back everything
Leaving nothing behind,
Without forgetting anything,
Because each departure
Is a blade that tears off
A part of my being
To offer it
On the altar
Of the god
Of voyages.

My Somali

Of this world you are the witness,
From the dust you question
The sphere of sky.

Limbs stripped of flesh,
on the edge of nothingness,
what image will you keep
of men, your brothers?

My Somali, fortunately
you cannot see yourself through
the television watching you.

Fortunately you are unaware of
This world,
Neither can you hear the laughter

Over the dinner table and wine,
Nor the excellent discourse
Which constructs a life over the tomb.

For you none of that exists,
Nothing but that land cursed
By the sun and the rain,
That soil once blessed by the gods
And today beyond the hope of man.
Perish, my brother,
Perish without regret,
Die in peace,
The world is so.

(1998)

Death to Immigrants

Me, I've arrived today.
And you? Yesterday? Day before?
Immigrant, from what country are you?

I come from Africa
Cradle of mankind,
I peopled this earth
At the mercy of storms.
Like the oceans
I follow the tide
Along the mild shore.

Immigrant, this land is not yours,
This country is mine, that of my parents,
This country belongs to –

Foreigner, out of my country,
Alien, sans-papiers, slit-eyes, nigger!
Me, I'm a real blockhead ...
French from Poland, from Russia, Spain,
Americans from Italy, Ireland or Senegal,
This land, is it Palestinian?
Is it Jewish, Arab or Berber?

You who are of today and chase those of yesterday,
Don't you get chased somewhere else?
We're all settlers of one place or another.
So then, immigrate. To death.

(2000)

Nkosi Johnson

You left in a burst of lightning,
After ten years of adult infancy
Like a question mark
Calling our world into doubt.

Child of the generations of hope,
Of the new world of Mandela,
Brought down under the banner of AIDS,
What impression do you leave for mankind
When your forebears were broken by apartheid
Bearing abortions and monsters
Continually devouring the entrails
Of dark South Africa?

Yet, when your voice thundered out,
Shame filtered down into the lairs
Of mean self-interest and indifference.

Behold how hope is rising now
Beyond the damnation of love
And the poverty of a bloodied continent,
Of its past and the future
Haunted by vampires.

Nkosi, blood of the blood of the blood,
Your voice may enjoy no spring,
But your breath is in the heart
Of a new fraternity without frontiers
Who make suffering an injustice,
Your offering our true conscience.

Nkosi, you were naught but innocence,
Sacrificed on the altar of the uncaring,
But still, your memory will bring hope
To the forgotten destiny of races.

Amir Mounib was born on Moheli, the smallest of the main Comorian islands, in 1981, and is a member of the Centre de Ressources there, which arranges an annual reunion of younger Comorian poets. He is fluent in five languages (French, English, Mahorais, Shicomori and Sakalava, the Madagascan language). He is currently pursuing his studies in Mayotte.

My High-prowed Sailing-boat

You, who from that first dawn
Have been built out of the tree's body,
With a cry of joy, ringing the alarm
Of the axe, the panga and sabre,
Their courage being their weapon,
O, daughter of green Bénara;

You, whom millions of generations
Have witnessed, have known you,
Whether Djumbé Fatima, Queen of Moheli,
Or the Sultan Andriantsouli of Mayotte,
I know you've lived through many civilisations;

O my sailer, no matter the weather
If it blows, if it thunders or if it pours,
You'll return through the long darkness always
With your world shining joyfully at meeting again
After such a long period of absence
From familiar eyes.

Adjmaël Halidi was born at Tsembehou in Anjouan in 1986. An article on his work in *Témoignages* (5 January, 2006) describes him as prolifically talented and unpublished, but known for having taken the clandestine route from his home country to a place of safety. Currently resident in Antananarivo, he is pursuing advanced studies under Serge Henri Rodin. As his work is uniquely compounded of double, and even triple, meanings, it is exceptionally difficult to translate. For instance, the title of the last poem, "Comoriâtre", means primarily "To be Comorian", but then secondarily "To be a bitch." The last line, "Oh! lie. Gare chie!" reads "Oh! tied, beware, tshi!", but also sounds "Oligarchy!" – and furthermore has the innuendo which could be rendered in another reading as "Back to bed, slut!" Here, out of a possible half dozen approximate versions, two are given. They were made independently of one another.

Evening Prayer

Islands
my Moon-isles
– while those baboons enrich themselves –
revive forgetfulness
just as life dies
as one admires dying
as one kills oneself in idle talk
as one dies while living
know, Islands of the Moon
my Moon-isles,
that it's neither the cock
that it's nor the horn –

this is no more than an evening prayer
driven by our bastard local dance:
the mgodro sakalava

Notes

(a) The moon is no longer the moon
    she is too hoary for a moon

(b) The contrary currents we love –
    but it's not our fault
    if we march in historical reverse

(c) The hills and the suns
    make our President a King …
    while our unmatched story
    continues to uproot in a vile History …

(d) We estimate you die only once
    (old Comorian saying)

Water like Gold / O Comoros

(To you like more / as a Moor,
seated at my sides / a marked man)

As was once predicted
your shores are burning, Comoros,
the crying out
of your Bantu forebears: *komoro* …
the Swahili alarm to watch out for the volcano.

Look at them! Your descendants fling
themselves off like a sycamore's fruit;
your daughters, gorgeous in their veils, no longer
in the abyss, they sparkle no more like gold / Comoros.
Your wounds run too severe.
What degrades this land like death / Comoros
so deeply
that your closest ones discharge:
"Our country can no longer deserve / Comoros
To be called Moon-isles?"

Written during the crossing towards Mayotte, June, 2002

To be a Comorian

"So many vain men sow mines!"

The intertidal zone is not the blood
where tripe peels apart –
such are the desiderata –
the stinking, vomited subjects
of the south …
sick of your rice / malnourished!
Flying ouch! / poultry! such the wings
mastering themselves start: stop, these clandestines,
such the perinatal setting on fire.
Word said / hunted: leavening!

Our own fluid
drained by our own faith / liver
frustrates:
one of those slaps! dance / independence,
such the seas the nerves

called by the foamy ticks / mosquitoes,
a shared court / crossing the backsliding sand.

... in the rhythm of dying of starvation
... in the rhythm of tempo / a skin theme
: Heap up the empty dung-beetle!

Cross / fly / hold
the raging waters; so cloned the mad celebrants
the stripping waters ... and nothing ...
only a shilling of spikenard / Bob Denard, at Mtsamboro
... legionnaires at eleven o'clock ... Sisyphus ...
the story repeats ...

: "others will come to save us / epidemics
laying waste the pittance we dreamed."
Oh! tied, beware, tshi!
Oligarchy!

Bitch of Comoros

"So many famines!"

Flippant these passers-by
Whose convictions flake off
Like desiderata
Bloody sputum
From the south
Poorly nourished!

Sluts! Salivating
Skies grab hold of the living
Like the foment that accompanies birth
Cursed: fermentation!

The flow untangles
Dries up, sometimes
Frustrating:
Indepen! dence
Like those mercenaries
Who buzz like mosquitoes
A new invasion of the land

… to the rhythm of lassitude
… to the rhythm of the tempo
: So as to fill the excremental void!

Twirling/pirouetting
Storms; cyclones of libation-bearers
United Nations … then nothing
Like a Bob Denard at Mtsamboro
… sea-serpents at eleven o'clock … Sisyphus …
Story told in reverse …

:"Other
epidemics
erode the hallucinatory support."
Back to bed! Slut!

(Translated by Carole Beckett)

MAYOTTE

Abdou S. Baco was born on Mayotte in 1965. After his education there and in Réunion, he was sent to France for further study. In 1991 he published the first Mahorais novel, which includes the rimed dedication to his father (included here), and in 1993 (also with L'Harmattan) he followed this with another, telling the growing up story of little Bana, who wishes to be a poet. Currently he is the director of Cultural Services in Mamoudzou, the chief commercial city, where he lives.

To My Father

You who far too soon left me.
You abide and you always will in the depths of me.
Without warning anyone you left us.
Your taking off, sudden and unexpected, affected me terribly.
You have preceded us on the route leading to only one place.
How I have wished to make that voyage at your side!
I'd like forever to be that little boy in a cap
    resting on your shoulders.
Like that day you took me to Bandrélé
to have me entered in the Civil Register of State.
You who tirelessly held converse with the spirits.
You who in the intimacy of night contemplated the stars.
You who for a ridiculous price warded off evil spells.
You who with your irresistible charm nearly lost an eye.
You abide and you always will in the depths of me.
The thousand scandal-mongers of M'Zoisia tried to separate us.
But we were the stronger.
Together we put up quite a struggle.
Together we fought off all slanderous talk.
And great was our hard-won victory.

When I think of you today I say to myself:
you are and will always be my true father.
When I think again of that day, the day of your sudden end
I shed smarting tears.
I honour the name of the Almighty, so that His peace be with you.
O you my father, man of magic!
How I'd like to taste once more your delicious cakes,
a reward among many others of your esoteric powers.
How I would like to hear you sing to the rhythm of tambours.
I would like deep in the crowd to see you dance.
I would like with their enthusiastic attention to watch you
    proudly displaying your talents in occult science.
But alas, that's all finished now!
You died your fine death, shrouded in your good earth.
Yet you abide still and always will in the depths of me.

First Love-letter

My dear Fléra,
I'm seated over here I am
Under the tree that covers the school
And I feel as if in a fairy-tale
That you belong to me that you're with me
But deep in my heart
It's like a heaviness
Which will bring on my tears
Because I cannot be your choice
I hear the cars which pass
Along so invitingly
And without awareness see
The branches of the tamarind swaying
It's like an interlude
Expressing my need to be alone

But all this really hurts me
Because always always I love
And often I ask when
Will the wind change direction
When will I meet up with
She who controls them
Who will lift me from this world
Which I find rather awful
And take me away to new shores
To an island more savage still
Where I'll know true happiness
And live on without distress
But oh well it's only a dream
That works on me day by day.
If only you would be my girlfriend
Dear Fléra my sweetness.
That would be immensely helpful
In tackling this ever so futile life.
Signed:
      Bana

Moussa Abdou's poem was a finalist in a competition held for schools in 1987, resulting in an elegant pictorial book on the subject of Mayotte's bangas, published in Mamoudzou two years later. Traditionally young adolescents of Mayotte are encouraged to build their own shacks away from the family compound, returning home only for meals; in these decorated bangas they may complete their homework and practise courtship procedures. This young competitor had perhaps been studying Jacques Prévert on the syllabus, for his poem is a witty variation on the French poet's "To Paint the Portrait of a Bird".

How to Endear Yourself to a Young Maiden

First of all build your own banga
with doors and windows that are open,
hang them with lacy curtains,
collect rare fruits, shiny and costly,
with roses and other sweetsmelling flowers
and play languorous music.

At the approach of the young maiden
Beauty should reign in your house.

Wait until she means to pass by,
place yourself at the door,
ready to give her a wink of the eye
which she'll understand and come.

If she does not enter
you didn't wink properly at all,
so you must wink with the other eye.

Horizontal or vertical,
cohabitation is convivial.

Nassuf Djailani was born in 1981 in Chiconi on the west coast of Mayotte and educated in Bordeaux in France as a journalist. He lives back in Mayotte, where he is the correspondent for *Kashkazi*, the inter-island weekly newspaper. His first collection of poems appeared in 2004, but the piece below is taken from the preface to his collection of poetic short stories, *Une Saison aux Comores*, published in 2005.

A Season in the Comoros

There was a time when there was one island, a few islands, four islands. Spewed out from the gaping throat of a mad volcano off the coast of the African sea. Rocked by marine currents, the foam of the vast Indian Ocean. Absent from historical manuals, from memory. Nevertheless there evolved here, in this shut off 374 square kilometres, a population, or rather populations come from the four corners of the earth. On the brink of independence, the people of the African continent said stop to colonisation. The important thing was national independence. And here, in the archipelago of the warring sultans, one voice, then two, then many said no – through the ballot-box – to the military detachments of the old colonial power.

"Stay French to be free," we read on the placards. So what was taking place? Historians and politicians on all sides offered their explanations. And what has happened since? Still conquered land, I'm talking of our own.

Land of anger
orphan,
brought forth in cosmic sorrow and rage,
creative fury,
explosions of inflammatory volcanoes
spitting out their burning lava,

forced Al-djazaïr l'kamaria,
from the depths of nothingness,
four stars arranged on the dorsal fin of the ocean
rocked by Mother Africa,
curled against her flank,
close by,
torn since its tender youth by shabby quarrels,
O my land!
forever separated from your Comorian sisters,
at the base of the Indian calabash,
a shining crescent,
watch how it grows larger, shines, draws nearer, enormous,
O my land,
you're no more than a gorging of promise,
but tomorrow you'll shine with all splendid fires.

 **Yazidou Maandhui** was born in Mayotte in 1983 and shuttles between the village of Labattoir on Pamandzi, near the capital of Dzaoudzi on Petite Terre, and Roussac in France, where he is completing his studies. His *Le Palimpseste du Silence, ou Le Silence des Dieux* of 2005 is the first volume of French-language poetry of commercial standard to be published in Mayotte (by Les Éditions du Baobab of La Maison des Livres).

The Pawpaw

Casually it balances
Under the caress of turbulent heat,
Rogueish under its splendid robe
Like a juicy bulb lighting up
In the peace of the countryside
This mango-papaya

Impatiently my belly grumbles
Jealously clasping its beauty
In my large squinting eyes,
I predict its taste, feel its texture
With the fingers of my desire,
Not to scratch it with awkwardness

In a fraction of a second a bat flies out
Taking only a mouthful

The Dream of a Naartjie

Dewy adamantine on a dangling filament
Innocent with the coolness of a stolen dawn
This gilded mandarin bursts with mourning
Sobbing for the lost essence of her fruitiness

The tart odour absorbed in your peel
Naartjie clasped in the hand
The pupil of your eyes in the palm of silence
I search the heavens for the words of your release

Clementine, O clementine
A blank page on which I draw you
Don't ever turn to the breath of oblivion
Fruitful under a suspended sky
In the tracks of the past a provocative sorrow
Bloodshot dusk which dreams of tomorrow

Dawn at Pamandzi

Dawn instils
A pouring of embers
Softened by haze

Flowing from your voice,
We share a tear
A few pearls of dew,
A herb-tea.

The perfume of souvenirs
The cinnamon of your sighs

Smoke of the cooking-pot
Our bodies bubbling
Pamandzi, I'm leaving you
Don't cry for our fate, sing

Stoke at our laughs, Mother
Worse than a bitter landscape
Are the tears on your face

Pamandzi, I'm leaving you
But just as sure
As the dawn will return
I will to you.

ISLAND REPORTS

Mauritius: From Dodos to Jumbos

Even the best maps miss out all or some of the Indian Ocean African islands, but for South Africans with a yen to suspend their regular travel routines in favour of luxuriating in a year round honeymoon landscape, Mauritius is very much there, already luring the avant garde of tourism – those who would rather find it for themselves than tramp the tyretreads of where the charabancs have been. Mauritius is close, not that dear to reach, English-speaking if you press hard enough (it was ceded to the British during the Napoleonic wars) and, best of all, the welcoming place it claims to be where travellers are still hail-strangers, not yet victims. But the number of tourists has quadrupled in the last eight years to 18 000. So be warned – the way the island is gearing itself to industrialise tourism now, the situation will not remain this pleasant much longer.

Mauritius from the air is like a phosphorescent sea of green – sugar-cane green, jungle green and savannah green – in a sea of euphrastic blue. Periodically dolorite breaks through like stone fingers out of a tapestry glove. The plane surfs in over more sugar-cane, the sweetest lawn in all the world. Hot air winds you as the aircraft door sucks back and in summer it's hot and humid right through from midnight to dawn. Right outside the airport are stupefying stretches of tropical and subtropical trees, and fruit, and flowers, and the lush scenic drives a mob of taxi-drivers competes to take you on right now. First thing you discover is that comprehensive tourist information on the island is not readily available – those glossy pamphlets are more like collectors' items you unearth later on, when you *know* where to go. Meanwhile trust the first taxi-driver who speaks functional versions of French, English, Creole, Hindustani, Urdu, Tamil or Arabic – he will adopt you.

Near enough to Plaisance Airport are two leading international hotels, Le Morne Brabant and Le Chaland (R6 to R10 for bed and breakfast, add about 20% for air-conditioning with mosquito nets included). Most visitors have little reason to venture into the hinterland, for it is a mood of comfortable inertia which blesses these hotels. Both are geranium-coloured concrete strings of beach bungalows scattered through acres of casuarina trees. Strolling through the undergrowth, along the intertidal zone and over black volcanic flagstones with the reward of an air-conditioned meal at the end of it, adds incentive to appetite – after days of flipping between the cordon of reefs and the white beaches of a warm, vapid, turquoise sea. Coral does burn, sea-urchins spike, but salt is a marvellous healing agent.

Mauritian food is varied, French more than just in name, recognisable and not the kind that sends you searching for Entero-Vioform. (It's the water that might get you, though.) Seafoods are cheap and plentiful – freshwater prawns called camarons are a speciality. Fish dishes served à la creole include an all-purpose curry and herb sauce that is worth bringing home by the bottle. Two local fish are the stonemouth and the dame-berry, both officially adjudged first class. A rarity is palmiste salad, made from the core of young palms – a party of six can happily demolish one tree between courses.

Dance-bands playing thin versions of "Ob La Di" on select evenings attempt to bring Sea Point to the tropics. That's the time to move to any of the other remoter hotels: the Touessrok on an isle of its own with ferry; the Park in the botanical garden of a sugar estate; the Mascareignes, named after Pedro Mascarenhas, Portuguese navigator – hence the Mascarene Islands, of which Mauritius with Rodrigues and their dependencies is one part and Réunion the other; the Blue Lagoon for England 'at home'; the Île de France, off the Yacht Club of the sheerly blue Grand Baie. The further you retreat from the tourist circuit, the lesser the prices for greater service. Over Christmas and Easter Mauritius is overbooked, but displaced visitors can quite safely resort to any number of pensions above filling stations or markets, where hospitality is modest but keenly welcoming.

Nowhere within an area of 30 x 40 miles can the bug-eyed traveller find more quantities of acutely varied cultures – European, African and Asian – co-functioning with what appears to be harmony and ease. The French and English, still behaving like the eccentric, sunburnt subduers of the mosquito that they are, live on in colonial houses of the sugar baron days, each landscaped like a little Versailles. Sugar is Mauritius's reason for living and accounts for 97% of its exports. The young private sector of the capital, Port Louis, hops to Johannesburg, Salisbury, London and Paris in a vigorous campaign to diversify the economy.

A habit one soon develops in that enervating climate is frequent stops at any hour at one liquor shop after another for raw rum drowned in Coke (one rupee) or, for the same amount, enough pawpaws, mangoes, pineapples, litchis, dates, coconuts and bananas, etc., to feed one South African for a week. A rupee is worth 13 c. Chinese gambling in the form of quatre quatre, which by the way is illegal, is a colourful way to pass the night. It is operated in brightly lit dens that one can't help noticing are police protected. The Friendly Place of Port Louis is where to go. Stakes start as low as 5 c. Drinks are on the house (watch the whisky which is cane-spirit with essence).

Mauritius falls under the scheme of the Indian Ocean Tourist Alliance (IOTA), which this month launches a many-pronged publicity campaign to speed up tourism and trade from Southern Africa to its four island regions. Package tours arranged by American Express (from R233 upwards) have operated through IOTA territory since November. Taking note of Morocco and the UAR earning R15 million a year each through tourism, IOTA is turning this way to the nearest industrialised country which 'exports' over 300 000 tourists a year.

Air Madagascar with Air Mauritius and SAA already flies a convenient weekly island hop from Durban to Tananarive and on. Symbolic of the Alliance's step into the colour-poster world of global tourism is the new Hilton, which should be operative in Tananarive in May. By 1974 Mauritius itself should be equipped for invasion sized parties from Europe when a tourist leg opens via the Seychelles for Jumbo 747s.

The only thing which is well and truly dead in this easygoing jungle is the dodo. Fated to survive only as an illustration of Darwinian theory, the Mauritian dodo was in fact clubbed to extinction during the Dutch occupation of 1638–1710, a period which saw the introduction of sugar-cane from Java and the deer, which is a hunter's delicacy to this day.

The island's curious Pieter Both, a vast boulder poised at 1 800 ft., commemorates a drowned Dutch sea captain. It was off Île de France, as the French christened it, that Napoleon's navy won their only battle against the British – and it is over those wrecks that scuba divers now trail bubbles in search of pieces of eight or luminous tiddlers for aquariums. The only battle which receives a retelling, though, is the landing of a world record 1 100 lbs. Pacific (*sic*) blue marlin off Le Morne.

Folklore had it that Pieter Both would topple when the British pulled out; it didn't. Folklore has to be adapted from the romantic past to an emergent present. The dodos are all gone, but the jumbos are coming.

(*News/check*, Johannesburg, 20 February, 1970)

Réunion: Landfall for a Stopover

To reach Réunion – 2 700 kms east of South Africa, right out there in the midst of the Indian Ocean – once took months on end through grey cyclonic weather. The Dutch explorers managed to make it, even before Van Riebeeck. Nowadays you merely board a UTA or SAA flight to Mauritius and climb off four hours later at the stopover before their final destination. You will feel slightly left behind on a desert island if your compatriots all fly on to their better organised honeymoon locale (everything prepaid). But there are reasons aplenty to disembark before them, here on Réunion.

For a start, there are no other tourists. This means that together with the island's inhabitants you will have the place to yourself. You can easily do the whole circuit in a car in one day. Buy a map, hire a vehicle. There are no guided tours. Only this: if you wish to drive yourself on Réunion, you have to be alert. The roads are one hairpin bend upon another. Daredevilry and courtesy will serve you well in turn.

And be warned: rum costs as much as Coke. With Coke at 30 c. a bottle, you may just as readily as most of the local population land below the poverty line. The most economical Oriental meal – pure rice, with sufficient bacon to remind you of a skimpy breakfast back home – will set you back R5 or more. Cinema R2.50 (double for *The Exorcist*). A naartjie (imported from South Africa), 18 cents. A postcard: 20 cents. So know that inflation lies ahead of you.

Once you compensate for that, you may relax. Here delight upon delight awaits you, since Réunion is one of the most spectacular, one of the prettiest places in the whole world – a fragrant island of perfumes, as the poets say, a favourite of the sun. Flowers, enormous and tropical, come into view like flying saucers. Flowers disrupt the traffic. Flowers choke up the pavements.

Indeed, this lavadump in the wide blue Indian immensity is known as the 'island of poets'; that is to say, many future poets enjoyed languid, luxurious formative years here, spending their working lives in Paris, only to return to have streets named after them and statues erected, holding lyres or frowning heroically and neurotically. Léon Dierx even managed to have the magnificent Musée des Beaux-Arts named in his honour.

In French literature Réunion has been what the Caribbean was to Shakespeare – a source of much authentic exoticism. The French-language poets of Réunion through the nineteenth century exported back to their motherland cargoes of juicy local colour; once over there themselves they suffered disillusioned reveries and nostalgia for their childhood wonderland. The effect of reading the total effusions over the island of the Parnassian, Leconte de Lisle, and a host of his imitators, is of eating too much fruit salad. My favourite is Louis Ozoux, a professor of medicine, born and died on Réunion and surely a slave, like all the other colonisers of his day, to metropolitan trends in writing. Yet by the 1920s he could generate some irony off his own bat to comment on their digestive torpor.

Currently the literary scene is in the hands of an islander aged twenty-two who publishes in the Réunion dialect. He is an engaging orphan, born of endless blikkiesdorp and perforce of cultural miscegenation. Alain Belair uses his own slummy backchat as an instrument of wit to subvert the imported product. He has never been to France and is the first person to publish a volume of poems in this style on the island itself. The rising interest in patois adaptations of the French of the academy, with the lexicons and scholarly grammars beginning to appear, signals the advent of an independent culture of great interest to South Africans.

You begin to understand life on Réunion when you witness their volcano. The whole island came into being thanks to this one vent. The base third of the island is actually still in the process of coming to rest, afflicted with drains of deadly gasses and burning magma. Above it is the sinister moon landscape, with streaks of raw metal and foul acid. Only desert plants cling on up here, between eruptions.

By contrast, Réunion's people are deeply friendly, but they do not mess with you. They do not beg. They also don't spend the whole day cleaning your shoes. They are beautiful people who allow you the space to behave just as well as they do.

So meet the Creoles. Creole is not an ethnically defining term. What it means these days is: born on the island. It also means that you find Creoles in every conceivable colour, from sugar baron down to water buffalo. On the other hand, the metropolitan-born whites, superficially welcome, are nicknamed 'les oreilles' – a bitter echo of the period when they branded imported slaves on their ears.

Catholic Creoles have not yet, as in the Republic of Mauritius, heard of family planning. Nor have the Muslim, Hindu, Buddhist and Protestant Creoles, either. Fifteen years ago Réunion had the world's highest figure for population growth. The consequences of this at present are somewhat frightening. Now that French health services have come to grips with malaria and smallpox as well, and the infant mortality rate has been reduced by fifty per cent, Réunion has as a result a population of which sixty per cent is under the age of twenty.

There is no room for more; there is no work for any more.

Despite the fact that Réunion is so near us and the rest of Africa, it is actually a part of Europe – to be precise, the last bit of the 97th department of France. With 150 years of colonial status and the Second World War behind it, the island is every bit as French as the Loire or Provence. It's just a smidgin of Europe Outre-Mer, or Overseas, as they say. Even the TV news on Réunion is identical to that seen at home every night.

This relationship has a stranglehold on the island, because it is dependent on France for everything. For all basic goods. Even the staple foodstuff, rice, is entirely imported from France. That is why most things are so costly. In exchange for its existence, all Réunion may give back to France is sugar and vanilla, as well as carnation essence which is used as a perfume base. Yet the island produces less than one third of what it costs to keep it going.

So now all the free Creoles can do, rather hopelessly, is dance the sega. The sega of Réunion is distinct from the sega of Mauritius, of Madagascar, the Seychelles or any of the islands of the Comoros group. To dance the sega, think of Harry Belafonte, put an extra 180 degree sway in your hips, carry your body like a cocky suitor, let out your deepest notes and you're back in slave days when the sega was forbidden as devil-music.

The sega subculture is strange and compelling; it alters the entire cosmopolitan tone of the island. Every Creole you come across, kitted out in his T-shirt and bell-bottoms, make no mistake about it, will answer you in the neatest French. But that accomplished, off he will slope into that impossible, fatalistic other world where there's no money, no jobs, no nothing, and where Creole is spoken.

Such is the miserable other side of this paradise, with its high percentage of human refuse, with its terrible malnutrition, about which all you can do is sing. At night the capital, Saint Denis, is dogs howling and the cough of tubercular children.

Now you look at the natural wonders with the eyes of survival. You notice how the coral reef on the west side of the island only just holds the Indian Ocean at bay to form a kind of shelter for the fishes which, like the flowers, come in every dazzling colour. You notice how the scenery around Hell-bourg or the Plaine des Palmistes must have the heaviest rainfall in the universe – the black, dried lava is simply overwhelmed in greenery, with bananas, avocadoes and cycads and more, thriving in rancid fruitfulness. Over violent precipices career a thousand waterfalls, one of which would reduce a Karoo farmer to tears.

On Réunion there is no segregation as such. All colours, all religious affiliations one way or another manage remarkably to come together – in their choirs, the army, in schools, in the university, in bed. Nor is 'Cafre' exactly a swear-word here. There is a charming village called Plaine des Cafres and to call a mop-headed doll a 'Cafrine' is no impoliteness at all; rather it is a compliment, suggesting earthy attractiveness.

Therefore all that the tourist on Réunion has left to fear is a cyclone. The worst in the twentieth century occurred in 1948, and the charmingly named Gervaise in the sixties ripped venomously right through the middle of the volcano itself. If the alert sounds and a cyclone approaches, duck into the nearest concrete building. Or stay in your Creole house with all its fine wooden fretwork, make everything fast and keep hoping for the best.

Your aeroplane will have to turn back. You'll sweat like a sponge, as you know that the damage a cyclone may cause is measured by Hiroshima standards. Cyclone season ends on the same day as summer each year: 15 March.

The return fare to Réunion from Johannesburg, for a stay of between a week and a month, is R241.80.

(*Rapport*, Johannesburg, 17 August, 1975, and 14 March, 1976)

Baudelaire Rounds the Cape

Charles Baudelaire was born in the year Napoleon died – 1821. By May, 1841, his step-father, "anxious at the dissipated life the young poet was leading in Paris" (as the chronology of the definitive edition of Baudelaire's works has it) was ready to dispatch him on a voyage to Calcutta. He was to escape loose women and the influence of Balzac and Nerval. The somewhat humourless step-father, General Aupick, a chevalier and officer in the legion d'honneur, was clearly distressed by his step-son's inclination to debauchery, both intellectual and sensual, and the Far East would provide, at least, distance from any literary career. On 9 June, 1841, the young Baudelaire, a minor without income, temporarily escaped debt and ruin by sailing from Bordeaux on a three-master cargo vessel of 296 tons, carrying mail and machinery and a few cramped passengers. Although some biographers maintain Baudelaire's own myth that he did indeed sail through all the gloryholes of the East, he in fact did not.

The Paquebot-des-Mers-du-Sud sailed for two months and twenty days with good wine on board, salted meat and dried vegetables, round the Cape off which a storm ripped out one mast (and Captain Saliz shot an albatross), through long, scalding tropical calms as banal as its quarters were squalid. Its first landfall was Île de France, or rather what had been the British colony of Mauritius since 1810. Bernardin de Saint-Pierre had landed at Port Louis on a similar journey round the Cape of Good Hope in the 1770s and with the publication of *Paul et Virginie* in 1788 had established Mauritius as the ideal location of Rousseau's romantic paradise. There pure love in lush natural surroundings, unaffected by the deformations of mass society, could flourish untrammelled; there savage nobility and gentility could preserve man in his goodness, a prey only to the damaging inhumanity of a civilisation that would shipwreck, just as the vessel that brought Virginia back from an enforced, rigid education in the metropolis had done. Between Saint-Pierre and Baudelaire had come the revolution, with the industrialisation of Mauritius into a sugar estate. Darwin and The Beagle had preceded Baudelaire in 1836 and the dodo, that Magellan and the Dutch East India Company had enjoyed clubbing, had been declared extinct.

Baudelaire visited the tomb of the legendary Paul and Virginia in the exotic gardens of Pamplemousses, where he spied an island-born beauty who occasioned the sonnet, "A Une Dame Créole" (to be his first published poem). He had in a "perfumed land" seen a "brown enchantress" who, if she were to grace the courtly landscapes of France, would germinate a thousand sonnets for every one that could be inspired by a stiff French madame. By 19 September he had acquired on Mauritius what for the rest of his life would be a stockpile of sensuous detail: the "odours" and "charms" of sea shanties, the tamarinds and mosses, the bulging fruit and floral decoration, the still, monotonous sun and an image of feline, womanly grace that would result in his choosing his mulatto mistress, Jeanne Duval, to whom his cycle of 1842–60 would be dedicated. (He eventually found her backstage in Paris; her role was of a servant and her one line on stage was the archetypal "Madame est servie".)

The Paquebot sailed for the French island of Réunion with Baudelaire on board, landing at Saint Denis. Landfall in the tepid, shark-ridden bay (he wrote home to his mother) was a matter of plunging perpendicularly down a rope ladder when the quayside appeared. Réunion was also the birthplace of the Parnassian poet, Leconte de Lisle, whose family on the island would be ruined by the abolition of slavery in 1848. And it was also the herbaceous border into which Évariste Parny was born; his *Poésies Érotiques* institutionalised orange blossom, melancholia and the carving of poetic slogans into the boles of the Mascarene palm. Parny also collected the indigenous folk songs of Madagascar which, even when Ravel set three of them in 1925 as "Chansons Madécasses", raised scandalised eyebrows – their themes were an unequivocal cry of liberty, and the indigenous man's advice to his fellows was: "Mefiez-vous des blancs", that is, anti-white war-cries, and the policy of clubbing any Bible-bearing new tyrants to death on the beaches of the Indian Ocean.

Baudelaire, who knew his Robinson Crusoe and Man Friday, also knew how to upset the master-servant relationship of a lavish and prosperous island culture. As a guest of a nouveau riche Réunion family he wrote, not of the crowded lagoons, the languid arbours of the municipal gardens or of the decorated wooden houses, propped between jackfruit and bougainvillaea, but a cautionary verse to his host's Malabari serving girl. His advice to her was to settle for servitude rather than the only other rank the port of Saint Denis could offer her, that of mariner's prostitute. By the time of Réunion Baudelaire had had his fill of French mercantilism; he cashed in his onward ticket for a return passage on The Alcide, which carried horses from Sydney to Réunion, and Baudelaire back to Bordeaux.

After sailing from Saint Denis in November, 1841, The Alcide hit the doldrums and a cyclone in the Madagascar basin. Such oceanic instability and prolonged, dry torture was Ancient Mariner territory, and Baudelaire, once more claustrophobic and severely oppressed by the crew's thuggishness and boredom, recorded that his albatross was lassoed in, bullied, maimed and systematically crippled by the commercial buccaneers' inability to let the romantic imagination alone to soar over and dominate the tempests of the southern seas. And it was also the Flying Dutchman zone, as a haunted Baudelaire, potential satanist and blasphemer himself, would pick up from his translations from the demonic Edgar Allan Poe, and whom one of Baudelaire's heirs like Laforgue would use later as a mock-heroic symbol of the plagues and pestilences of trade and the irredeemability of those courageous enough to be exiled by God.

On 4 December The Alcide put in at Table Bay. Archival research reveals nothing of Baudelaire's five-day stay at the Cape, but there are the odd clues in the prodigious amount of work that he was to publish in the remaining twenty-six years of his life. "The Orient [he would write] smells of musk and cadavers. There are tropical isles that smell of roses, musk or coconut oil. The Cape smells of sheep." He refers to the wine of Constance, which should not be glossed as wine from the Lake Constance region, but as the Groot Constantia sweet liqueur red that his ship's captain exported to France, that C. Louis Leipoldt would try and recreate, and that would become one of the reputable French after-dinner delights, as in the sub-Baudelairean dandy's cellars of a character like Des Esseintes (in Huysmans's *Au Rebours*). The context in which the reference occurs is a negative one (something that Leipoldt fails to mention): in "Sed Non Satiata" Baudelaire would prefer the intoxicating breath of his "bizarre deity", "brown as the night", his "ebony-thighed sorcerer" to Constantia wine or, for that matter, opium.

But the visions of a magnificently rich and full-bodied African continent are there: "when my desires set off for you in caravan, your eyes are the reservoirs where all my anxieties may drink." This generalised and unknown Africo-Oriental-exotic hinterland yet to be laid bare becomes a common metaphor for ecstasy, oblivion and escape. He was to fantasise – and lie about – such subcontinental experiences frequently.

There would not be much point in trying to claim too hard that the Cape played some significant role in the formation of the first modern European poet. Yet, since he never travelled out of Europe again once he had returned on 15 February, 1842, despite lavish advertising to the contrary, one might assume that between the 4th and 8th December, 1841, whatever experiences bore down upon him would have left some useful impression.

His invitations to a voyage are always to be flushed with the psychedelic landscapes and erotic minutiae that balance his splenetic portraits of European urban squalor. His perverse flaunting of antiheroic journeys to hell and beyond, his artificial paradises and limbos, incorporate perfumed exotica with constantly recurring predictability. The odium and scorn he reserved for the bourgeoisie and petty officialdom, and his systematic moral subterfuge, bad manners, his flamboyant dedication to highly modulated sensual saturation and, above all, his recognition that outcasts, the beggars and lepers, the criminally inclined and the hanged – all pariahs – were *his* people, are hardly likely to make him a favourite household poet in the Cape today. He remains, in fact, 135 years later, the perfect antipoet in terms of current South Africa. He stands, in effect, amongst other things, for fruitful transgressions of the Immorality Act, a glorification of natural Black Africa, etc. He was a divine terrorist who didn't much care and who, like Gauguin, merely sailed on.

(*Contrast*, Cape Town, Number 39, April, 1976)

Cruising Off-shore

On 8th December, 1990, I set off on a luxury cruise with my elderly father. We shared much good humour about it being our 'last trip' together – a rather extravagant way for us to avoid a glum Christmas, unattended by the few immediate family we have left. We would have 400 fellow passengers with whom to celebrate the occasion aboard the MTS Odysseus of the Epirotiki Line, hired for the trip by a South African tour organisation. If we found no soul-mates aboard, at least we would escape the rest of the passengers and four meals a day at our frequent scheduled landfalls off the East Coast.

These were exotic places we had hardly heard of, where parties of such cossetted adventurers had in some cases seldom landed before, and in one instance never would again. Tourist information on where we were destined was not readily available, although this farflung archipelago is to South Africa what the better developed Caribbean is to Europe and the United States. Fistfuls of dollars would speak in the Indian Ocean, too, for this was the currency that spun the roulette wheel in the heaving casino and just about everything else. The trip had something to do with South Africa's emergence as a power in the region as well.

The last time my father sailed from Durban, Port Natal, was in 1941 to defend another empire. He was on a troopship called the Mauritania which was soon enough strafed by a Vichy-supporting plane from Madagascar. Four years later he returned home on the same vessel to discover his son. After half a century that son really had little sense of the anxieties his father was reliving; *mines*, those were the ones he was still afraid of. I had to reassure him all mines must have been swept from harbour mouths by now.

Our first port of call was still on the mainland: Maputo, the capital of war-torn Mozambique, now reduced to being one of the poorest countries in the world (together with Madagascar). On Sunday 9th we steamed there with our twin screws through Delagoa Bay. Formerly known as the Portuguese playground of Lourenço Marques, the

Transvaal that is wrapped around it would spill in for stripshows about the railhead. The neon signs have not been repaired since.

The only welcoming pizzazz these days is ABAIXO O APARTHEID stencilled on the derelict warehouses, and plugs for MARXISMO and LENINISMO which have evidently brought all around to incapacitation. Since Frelimo marched in to occupy the Radio Clube fifteen years ago, broadcasting the end of half a millennium of decadent European oppression and exploitation, the harbour has not been maintained. Each drooping crane would cost a small fortune to derust. Kept just functional by South Africa, the harbour closes between dusk and dawn; the team flies home every night to feel safe.

The highest building in Mozambique is a thirty-three-storey skyscraper, the ten top floors of which were never connected up or glassed in; they are occupied by squatters who have no way to dispose of refuse other than throwing it out on to the dismantled mosaic pavements. The Radio Clube, which used to house the pirate commercial LM Radio, is a heap of corrugated iron. Below it the late Samora Moses Machel the liberator, cast in bronze in his dapper Mao jacket, points the way from the Botanical Gardens not into the hinterland, but to the old Gil Vicente cinema which *still* shows dubbed American movies. Below that the drivers of refrigerated trucks, the new cowboys who make it through in convoy, despite the civil war with Renamo, wait to offload tons of frozen chickens on the Monday when presumably life will begin again. Meanwhile, the old grand-prix circuit is reclaimed by random maize-planters, and that's where one goes for a roasted cob.

There is now no paint factory or glass supplier in Mozambique, so every building is peeled down to a grim patina and open to the tropical weather. Only Embassy Row is maintained, mansions like prisons with aerials reaching up for Cuba or Zambia; South Africans have their trade bunkers, too, designed like fall-out shelters. Outside them women sell individual lumps of coal in tins.

The old-timer South Africans are stricken, recollecting the days when at this outdoor café one gorged bigger piri-piri prawns than at that one, washed down with Laurentina beer. At least the Polana Hotel where they used to weekend has been maintained as a sort of colonial museum, where foreigners in plain dress still may select the odd cake from a silver tray.

From there I manage to phone my friend, José Craveirinha, the finest poet in Southern Africa, only some of whose work has been translated into English from Portuguese. When we last met, at a conference of African writers in Rome, as one thoughtlessly does on such neutral ground he had invited me to visit him. Now, although only a few miles of potholes apart, we obviously could not meet physically. He was too old, he was ill, there were no taxis, his friend's car had broken down … worse still, he had stopped writing; he did not wish to talk about poetry. This was the Craveirinha who has spent years of his adult life in prison, under the old regime and then under the new, for insisting on writing too much. A year before, as patron of Maputo's organisation of poets, writers and artists, he had written an open letter to our new state president appealing for a stop to the genocidal destabilisation exerted on Mozambique by South Africa's warlords. He used this metaphor: "We are sailing in a ship that starts in South Africa and ends in Mozambique, floating in the same waters under the same stars. We are subject to the same tides, the same winds, the same tempests. And the same calm."

Now our literal ship was tied to his crumbling wharves. No wonder he would not come aboard for a cocktail under any circumstances; there were more lights burning on the MTS Odysseus than in the whole of his capital city.

The first and last monument seen from seaward in Delagoa Bay is the shell of a mammoth hotel – the Four Seasons, now called the Forty-one Seasons. This hollow monolith got off the ground on wrong foundations and may never be completed or demolished. Before it tribesmen wade out with nets, surer of traditional employments.

After three days at sea: Anjouan (a corruption of the Dutch name, San Johanna), the third of four islands of the Independent Republique Federal Islamique des Comores, where our elegant liner is welcomed to Mutsamudu container depot by the Arab school committee in their long white kanzus, lined up, dancing to tabors and flute. We are to be raced around the island like prisoners, driven by the military in clapped-out Peugeot trucks. These are decorated nevertheless in hibiscus and other trailing tropical flowers. The old connection from South Africa through LM to the Comoros was from one slave barracoon to the next; now it is the Coca-Cola route, with aluminium cans marked 'Keep South Africa Tidy' crunched in every alleyway. (Pepsi-Cola comes from Saudi Arabia.)

The French who imported most of the ancestors of these Muslim bodies turned the slopes of the sultan's volcano into the sweetest smelling outcrop on earth. Anjouan still produces most of the perfume-base of Europe; barrels of essence are flown out to Grasse. Notable is the ylang-ylang, pollarded to shoulder-height – a spreading tree that droops into blossoms like calamari, distilled in antiquated alembics to produce what used to be called macassar oil. When we heave into a plantation, the island's few proprietors take off on Vespas. The trees are festooned as well with bootlaces (vanilla-pods).

We are not taken to the Coelacanth Museum, but the fact is that off the east of Anjouan in 1952 Professor J. L. B. (Fishy) Smith of Rhodes University identified the common ancestor of all mammals, the fish that climbed out of the slime, thought to have been extinct since that puzzling event. However, here this hundred-pound four-legged monster still 'walks' about the local shoals, reminding the human intelligence from what gawping, greasy frame it is descended. Scuba-divers may be licensed to re-encounter their roots at the Hotel de Ville. Anjouan currently receives other foreign revenue from Kuwait, and – given the circumstances – Kuwait's assistance has been suspended.

A last transaction as the ship pulls out: Comorian boys lobbing tin trinkets and perfume samples on to the afterdeck and the crew firing back toilet rolls and cakes of soap.

On 14th December we anchor at dawn off Aldabra, an outlying speck of the Seychelles group. Aldabra is the largest coral atoll in the world, being twenty miles long, and as a plaque over the lagoon proclaims, "this wonder of nature is a gift by the people of the Republic of Seychelles to all humanity". It is kept as a sanctuary: no cigarette butts, no plastic waste. The Aldabra ring has a depleted population of protected giant tortoises, which used to feed sailing ships, and some of which survive from the Napoleonic wars which shaped the region. They brouse and breed with numbers on their shells that used to be made into shoehorns. This is also the teeming breeding ground of seabirds that rarely touch land otherwise, and some species are endemic.

We arrived from the elegant mother ship in a fleet of what flat South Africans call 'rubber ducks' (and the Americans glorify as Zodiacs), with hampers of Christmas cheer for the few humans, with lettuce to fortify the tortoises and bread to lure the tropical fish. That would be a fine way to be taken: with nose in a face-mask and teeth gripped about a snorkel, dandling one's body over the coralline display. Our party of bird-watchers is in a similar ecstasy as frigate-birds overhead frenziedly dive-bomb flat-footed boobies, which regurgitate in terror in mid-air to their benefit, and which in turn dive-bomb the poor fish for more.

Aldabra's little settlement of Picard (population seven men and one woman) is there to man a weather station. It includes a wooden Catholic church and a clubhouse with the best-read paperback library in the world: mostly Hammond Innes and, of all things, a fat biography of Saint Augustine of Hippo which some ornithological tagging team must have left behind. Nelson, the ex-softball champion, trained as a meteorologist in Nairobi, takes me to see the armful of giant crab they have caught for lunch, but somehow in all the excitement it has escaped the cook with his machete. What does Nelson do when he's not filing his four-hourly reports on sun, wind and rain? "Watch the sharks coming in, and out, of the lagoon with the tides." (An Aldabran joke.)

While we wait on the bleached shore in the warm rain the news comes over the radio from Mahé that we may land (since we have already landed). But the Seychelles government is sensitive about the damage so many of us may cause to the ecosystem and, despite the huge landing fee, we are the last cruise ship to have such permission. When Aldabra was part of BIOT (the British Indian Ocean Territories) it was close to being rented out to the United States during the Cold War to be concreted over as a supply base for aircraft-carriers; Diego

Garcia in the Mauritius group was chosen for that strategic purpose instead.

Thank God Aldabra survived, because it is true: the birds are fearless of humans. I slump in the heat against the bole of a casuarina, watched by a pop-eyed fairy tern three feet away. A dazzling red fody picks through the detritus of needles, moving between my coral-hopping sneakers. I slide a foot across and the bird moves into the space, glances at me, continues. Mauritius had its dodo, synonym for 'dead' and for 'dumb', which waddled up to greet men and was clubbed where it stood; the Seychelles had its sort of roc and the solitaire; Madagascar, the island subcontinent where evolution took extraordinary turns, had the largest extinct bird of all, weighing half a ton – the aepyornis. All clubbed down. Aldabra is the only place I know where one may be a birdwatcher without binoculars. It is chastening to think that nature once really was unafraid of us.

We make our stately arrival two days later at the central Mahé, with its smallest capital in the world, Victoria. Since independence this Commonwealth country, entirely created by the empire as a dumping ground for freed slaves and political prisoners, which has hardly yet published a written piece of literature in English – blissfully adrift from any of the mainstreams of the planet – has worked out a most successful socialist economy. This is based on copra production, deep-sea fishing and tourism of the honeymoon paradise variety for foreign exchange. The contrast with the other three socialist republics (Mozambique, Comoros and Madagascar) could not be more extreme. Everything on Mahé is in good nick; no attempts at skyscrapers, either, as some wise man decreed that no building on the Seychelles should compete with the palm trees in height. The grands blancs are mostly departed, leaving behind paint and glassworks, the Seybrew Breweries and a racially integrated society to admire.

President Albert René, who took over in a coup from playboy Sir James Mancham in 1977, happens to be landing from his pleasure-craft as our towering liner is made fast. Preceded by an over-excited military escort, his stretch Volvo circles and heads for his residence up in the cool mountains before we can get the gangway down. We arrive in time for the end of the inter-island Sunday soccer: Seychelles versus Réunion, under 16s, and the defeated locals cordially troop out of the stadium, leaving not a bottletop or sweetwrapper behind. (Most of the police are women, too.)

Recently the Seychelles hosted an international Creolophone conference, devoted to considerably more than delicious fish dishes and the sega dance-form. Creole representatives with French as a lexical base, particularly from the Caribbean, attended, with poets like Édouard Maunick as spokesman. 'Creole' here is a stretched, mixed style, for everyone born in the Seychelles is a Seselwa Kreol: included are the wooden and corrugated-iron kaz (cases – dwellings) and the wide-verandaed plantation mansions as well, approached along hurricane-lopped avenues of palms – in this landscape, Mascarene palms with their green sheaths. 'Creole' is a humorous love of over-description – roads on the Seychelles are not 'repaired' but 'rehabilitated' – and Joe Samy may sing of "Ozordi la fet" with unaffected patriotic sweetness.

Kreol Seselwa is spelt phonetically and the literacy primers produced by the Creole Institute are a delight: try *Alis dan Pei Mervey*, which gives an altogether enchanting 'dimansyon' to Lewis Carroll. The process began at the Mission Lodge in the mountains where children of slaves were taught trades under dragon's-blood trees by Anglicans and then came down to find no work on the Catholic shore. There a belvedere was built for Her Majesty the Queen to admire the sheer tea-bearing slopes, the winding flight of the tropic birds and the prospect that since the Seychelles, after six attempts, was finally ceded to the British in the 1820s, low-church English culture has made hardly any impact. So God bless she lives that house (a Mahé joke about Queen Elizabeth II in Buckingham Palace).

Kreol punctuation may be seen to hold ghastly historical traces: º * " " – these, as I learn in the spick-and-span National Archives, where none of their history is lost, are the brand-marks of proprietorship inflicted on their forebears. The following stands for pain and possession: (temples).

Most slaves on the Seychelles were called Mozambiquers or Madagascars, though I find that the last liberated black to die on Mahé

– at the age of approximately 110, in 1956 – had the name of Mrs Alice Japhet. An altogether different Alice story. Her African name was Atikulu. Her origins were South African. She was captured in a raid by Basothos in the Drakensberg, shipped out of LM in an Arab dhow, overtaken by a British cruiser and diverted here. Trained as a nanny, she was married off to either the facetiously named César or Pompé or Hannibal in the 1860s, who like her came from God knows where. She died, retired, in Anse Royale, never having returned to her 'grande terre'. She was branded with an exclamation mark down her cheek. Stories like these are unremembered in South Africa, still real in the world of Sesel. More than a tale of sewing seashells on the seashore.

Yet today – for all its rightful hostility towards the bastion of racism – for its food supply the Seychelles is sixty-eight per cent dependent on South Africa. Shops are stocked with South African imports from Paarl Perlé wines through butter and jam to skin-lighteners (banned in South Africa) and hair-straighteners with instructions in Afrikaans. In 1981 South Africa utterly disgraced itself by trying to secure an even greater part in the economy by hiring mercenaries to stage a coup against René. The aggressors were foiled, farcically sentenced to a life of more or less perpetual fishing thereafter. Somehow the upshot was an extended runway at the airport, for the cargo planes to move in instead.

We are towed to anchor between the next most beautiful isles, Praslin and La Digue. Following some complicated Victorian exegetical theory, the former was officially made the site of the original Garden of Eden by General Gordon, a few years before he miscalculated at Khartoum as well. His reason was the brazen nut of the coco-de-mer palm, now the republic's biggest tourist draw. This nut is the size and shape of the adult female human pelvis, fleshed out with moulded buttocks and a vaginal opening adorned with wiry pubic hair. Visitors to the Vallée de Mai can only stand aghast as well at the nut's opposite number, a male catkin which dangles in a state of semi-erection, dripping with honey that green geckos and sunbirds pick at all day long.

Opposite, on La Digue, some of the *Emmanuelle* movies were filmed … so erotic displays are a very public affair in the Seychelles.

On my wobbly hired 12-speed Puma, which had neither brakes nor the advertised gears, and was about as physical a challenge as I could master on the vehicle-less isle, I found in the Catholic church a notice imploring both 'mariens' *and* 'pariens' to accompany their offspring to the Christmas mass-baptism, so breeding proceeds quite pleasurably there, too. La Digue is also the home of the local paradise-flycatcher, which has not fared so well (only twenty pairs left) and which I could not locate. Chain-saws were buzzing at the venerable takamaka forest which is its last refuge. But ... from these wonderful trunks the necessary pirogues are carved.

Several of the other Seychelles islands are indeed bird or marine reserves. Bird Island to the north is the breeding ground of millions of sooty terns, which we spent most of a day watching scoop up an entire shoal of fish. The swell was too rough to land. At Curieuse – named after a ship by castaways who survived and prospered there – we inspected the ruins of the leper colony and the old turtle farm instead.

Besides being charming, Seychelles guides are well trained. On Curieuse while in awe of a granite outcrop pleated by water action into pink curtains, feet in a mangrove swamp, I first heard from one of them about the 'biscuit theory' of the islands' origin. Once when the ur-continent of Gondwanaland snapped like a dry biscuit into the landmasses of Africa, Madagascar and India, these were the granite crumbs left on the ocean floor. Volcanoes rose from the angry depths to surround them, each duly encircled with coral crowns.

The last of the lost atolls we visited was Farquhar (population twenty-five) south of the Amirantes, which on the Portuguese navigators' route to Goa – according to their poet, Camoens – were the real home of Venus. If breasty coconuts spouting milk are any guide, this is so. Named after a later governor, 'Faqa' is a well-ordered plantation staffed by labourers who at the end of the lopping season are airlifted out with their produce. Method of cracking coconuts for their yielding flesh: bowl them individually against the wicket marked on the storehouse wall – an interesting reversal of the fairground coconut-shy. After an over of that, retire to the shore of pulverised brain-coral under a wide straw hat. Actually, the sand is formed by parrot-fish which crunch up the slow-growing reef in their search for algae, and literally defecate beach ... Crazy place, Faqa ... That bright blue streak is a whale-road for humpbacks, stretching up to the Equator ...

Our last stop is 'historic' for us, at Nosy Be – big island – off the north-west of huge Madagascar, and a French protectorate from 1840 until independence. Historic, because for fifteen years all of the 'Red Isle' has been closed to Westerners. One day in October our state president flew in once again to Madagascar to conclude a trade pact aimed at restoring their economy; he was back in Pretoria for dinner. The upshot: an influx of skin-lighteners, hair-straighteners, Omo and Coke, plus an invasion of us luxury tourists on 22nd December, 1990, with fistfuls of Malgache ariaries that may not be spent anywhere else.

The crumbled, rutted town of Nosy Be – rusted one-time French provincial – is only too aptly named Hell-Ville. My advice to successors: carry a fistful of ballpens, which may be exchanged with schoolkids for foot-long chameleons, packets of peppercorns or brilliantly printed cotton cloths. In Hell-Ville the raised tombs of the dead, surrounded by zebra plants, are in better shape than some of the shacks of the living. Even a customs official whom I thought would protect me from predation broached the big question, his eye on the pen stuck in my notebook: did I have a 'stylo' for him; there was a shortage of writing instruments on Nosy Be.

While at the Hotel Venus in Hell-Ville I was being accosted by a bouncy Malayo-Polynesian in dreadlocks with the greeting, "Guten Tag", and an invitation to share a Three Horses Beer ... my more naturalist father had chosen to visit Nosy Komba, the opposite isle, which is a lemur reserve. There he evidently found his healing, his one memory of the trip that supersedes all those of his war: pouty-faced aye-ayes crawling up his safari-suit, probing their banded mandibles into the banana he proferred, their well-articulated hands patting his stubble, almost as slowly as the slow loris. Peacetime.

The only homework I did re Madagascar was plough through *Robert Drury's Journal* of 1729, which may or may not have been edited by Daniel Defoe. For fear of what I would find there I had been putting off the task for years. Held in captivity for fifteen years himself as a white slave by the Sakalavas, amongst whom I now was, Drury not only survived but also came of age intact, much married and respected as a sport of nature. But for him there lies no moral in his own tale, as on his escape he immediately sets sail for Natal where he "traded for slaves, with large brass rings, or rather collars, and other things. We bought in a fortnight's time seventy-four boys and girls. These are better slaves for working than those of Madagascar, being stronger, also blacker."

Defoe had no comment to make on this moral anomaly, unless his condemnation is hidden in an irony too deep for me to find. Remember, then, that in the West before the emancipationists human life and limb overseas had no value whatsoever beyond its capacity to labour. At least in the Seychelles they have discontinued the slave-crops: cotton, cinnamon, lemon-grass, cloves, pepper, vanilla ... Here in Madagascar they are *still* about all that is on offer.

Our last port of call we missed, on Christmas eve, owing to the vagaries of tide and time. We were too late to see more than the surf over Bassas da India by three hours, because Bassas da India – surely one of the world's most lonely places – shows itself in the middle of the Mozambique Channel only briefly when it is low tide in that realm. Treasure-hunters pay fortunes for licences to search there. To that disappearing isle, it turns out, ships have been lured for millennia – the recent wrecked trawlers that serve as guano-traps, perched upon it, the British wrecks, the French, the Dutch, the Portuguese, the Arabs and – before them all – the mighty Pacific longboats that first settled the neighbouring steamy shores. How's that for an untold story of the dawn of seafaring, omitted from the records of our Graeco-Latin heritage?

Kazantzakis in his sequel to *The Odyssey*, I suddenly remembered, had extended the European known world down this coast, had Odysseus dying at the Cape, facing Antarctica – a mythological titbit not likely to make much impact on the thoroughly automated bridge of our vessel, even if it was named after the great Western explorer himself. But our captain responded in a most moving way to this geographical hallucination of trawler hulks jammed in the middle of waste, sinking in the dazzling breakers beneath thunderheads. He had us line up on deck to drink a toast of iced ouzo, while he blew the mournful hooter in salute of lost seafarers.

Afterwards there was much dispute as to which European power Bassas da India belonged. According to the Admiralty charts it is part of metropolitan France, for two hours twice a day. Our resident conjurer had no illusion to beat that. Almost as bizarre as singing "Jingle Bells" at 32° to a musty piano accompaniment in the cocktail bar before a plastic fir.

I spent time on the lower aft deck late at night, in the cool, while the disco raged elsewhere, undergoing my own cure: listening to the Seselwa once they got off dishwashing. One real griot – rather, a Queequeg, a most gentle giant but surely a devil with a harpoon – gave epic recitals of how his dear Senegalais friend and fishing-mate came to grief. Twice I heard him do the bit about his friend's dismemberment while fallen off the ship. Our eyes popped at the gruesomeness of his last moments. Waving for help with his remaining arm, he had that taken as well, as the devouring hammerhead leapt into air, jaws open. None of the younger ones could top that for drama; in defeat they threw the last of our 20 000 empty Castle beercans into the phosphorescent wake and shook their heads sombrely at the injustice of the world.

Our griot's conclusions about life as a migrant fisherman on the factory ships that suck up tuna in these parts: the Spanish won't stop for a man overboard; the Brittany French will, but never cease complaining about it; the Japanese stop, but dock the pay; the Russians stop, but fine the retrieved more than their salaries. And the South African factory ships? They bring their own shark-fodder, don't hire Seselwa.

Lower in the Mozambique Channel from which South Africa's bad weather emanates we are hit by a force eight gale. Rollers rise to and slap over the bridge. Our cabin is like the inside of a washing machine. The lavish dining saloon is sparsely attended. The air-conditioning has recycled so many germs we all have sore throats, too, through which it is hard to vomit.

Dawn breaks at last over Durban, stacked like Miami on the African dunes. When we left eighteen days before thousands of fishermen of all kinds and ages were hoping to reel in a few marked fish out of the murky harbour and win some fabulous prizes. Now this access to the cruel regional power is very bleak, 'turbulent' as the politicians say in a violent land. To the Seselwa clutching their miserable tips it is the magic supermarket of their dreams. To us it is – well, the modern world.

Our disembarkation was hurried, as the MTS Odysseus had to transform itself for its next leg and its next task – as a hospital ship in the Gulf. Sounded familiar to my father.

(*Wasafiri*, Canterbury, Number 14, Autumn, 1991)

Promenades on Mayotte

Where lies an island in the shape of a sea-horse, protected by a coral reef forming one of the largest lagoons in the universe? Where do the brown beaches, ground out of old volcanoes, encircle it, with next to every second tree offering some tropical fruit? And the fruitbats dangling in the branches? And lemurs jumping between them? And the incredible green, incredible blue? Mayotte is the answer.

Mayotte is an island of only 375 square kilometres of dry land, but its boundaries include another 185 kms of that reef, which in turn holds in the 1 500 square kilometres of lagoon. With an average year-round seawater temperature of 30° C, this is one immensity of diver's delight. Indeed, by government decree many segments of the reef are sanctuaries today, where snorkelers laze alongside sea-turtles (no hitching rides), race sporting dolphins, scan for the last dozen or so dugongs or discover further sandy islets. When the whales come in to birth in August, this is a national event.

Mayotte is situated directly between the north of Madagascar and the African mainland, forming the fourth and last of the Comoros archipelago. This is the island which, in 1976, elected not to join their confederation, preferring to remain the colonial outpost of France. Technically a 'collectivité territoriale', Mayotte is the junior partner of Réunion Island, the far better funded French department to which it defers. Both enjoy the same TV schedules as the old motherland every evening, only an hour or two behind, although in other ways they could not be more apart from their European overlords.

The population of Mayotte is another phenomenon, be it said one of the most amicable, if poorest, in the world. The official census of 1963 rated it at 23 600, formed from the remnants of Bantu occupants of the eighth century, of Indonesians now called Austronesians of the tenth and of the overlapping Shirazi of Persia bringing the Muslim religion in the twelfth century. One outdated guidebook I consulted (of 1976) gave the total figure as 41 000, the next of 1980 as 70 000, with the current statistic amounting to 160 000. In other words the flourishing inhabitants of this lost enclave have managed to multiply themselves sevenfold in forty years. They call themselves 'kashkazi', which means fertile.

But partly the explanation is the influx of so-called clandestines from the other islands. They come by canoe, particularly from Anjouan, only 60 kms away, or by outboard from looming Nosy Be on the other horizon. These are the imperial power's migrants 'sans papiers', illegals comprising no less than one third of the people. The Foreign Legion here is deployed specifically to transport these unfortunates back whence they came, yet meanwhile the refugees keep the plantations harvested. On Mayotte you will rarely meet an indigene, and if you are a tramping tourist there's a word for you too: mzungu.

To hand I had an old copy of *The State*, published in August, 1912, when the fresh Union of South Africa was networking out along the Indian Ocean Rim to test the opportunities for trade and tourism. With haunting pictures, Mayotte features there as the choice destination and entrepot, to be reached by sea courtesy of Messageries Maritimes. Then Mayotte was rated as the most able and amenable landfall before Suez. Its exports included vanilla, palm-oil, copra and sisal, all outmoded nowadays in favour of the essence of the ylang-ylang tree. Its floppy, greasy blossoms are distilled in great tubs to form the basis of all scents.

But here is how *The State*'s awestruck reporter went overboard at his gorgeous landfall:

Let me try to describe Mayotte of the Comoros, approachable by a course winding among rocky volcanic islands green with forest from sea to summit. Set between green forest and blue sea are coves and beaches that invite one to become subjects of Neptune, content to spend the days in fishing and bathing, while the eye is refreshed and sight filled with the beauty of lights and tints on wooded hill and sea. In due time, no doubt, these wondrous spots will be discovered by pleasure-seekers from Africa, when it is known what lotusland here awaits occupation.

Eighty years later this discovery had not yet been made by many South Africans, it seems, as in *Getaway*'s theme issue on the Indian Ocean Islands is a mere mention as an awkward annexure of the more accessible Comoros. By then South African Airways was flying to Moroni direct. But now the situation is reversed: Air Austral's weekly flight out of Johannesburg (via Réunion) may land you any day you wish on Mayotte, the rest of the islands being out of reach.

When one of those giant Boeings comes in over its destination, the land to which the airstrip is attached lies prone like a basking manta-ray. At the rudimentary airport building of Pamandzi, do not expect modern facilities such as a Bureau du Change. You will be stepping back in time to the days when women with painted faces, dazzling in their lambas, sing the craft in. Clapping bamboo rattles, they ululate loudly and sweetly. Children storm to the fence from a thousand very modest dwellings and gawp. If you have family to greet you safely back, you will be leied about the neck with a chain of bougainvillaea and every other blossom.

Then there is the shared taxi experience. You will clatter out of there, the entire island being crossed to Dzaoudzi for one euro in ten minutes. Dzaoudzi is a sort of rock of Gibraltar, which the French purchased from a Malagasy sultan in 1841, ruling the entire island-chain securely for over a century from there. Still it is their military intelligence base, with a museum in formation, complete with old weapons and piles of cannon-balls.

But so far you have glimpsed only Petite Terre, and will have to return to tramp to the rim of its sulphurous, circular lake filling the old crater, or scale down to its mangrove cays over the weekend, as everyone else does, with a basket for a bask, watching the tropic-birds rise and dip. The main island, inevitably called Grande Terre, lies ahead and you are about to experience the principal activity of sweet Mayotte: ferrying back and forth between the two. A one-way voyage is free, but on the return you pay double, which you soon come to feel is logical.

The half-hourly ferries take all: bunches of bananas and other produce going both ways, backpacks, scooters, cars, horned zebus.

The Mahorais people, as they choose to call themselves, have invented a French verb for this activity: 'barger', to connect up easily. These 'Salama Djema' traversing the lagoon of Mayotte are breezily cool and the name means: Bon Voyage. The centre of the landfall on the other side is called 'Caribou', which means: Welcome.

To be frank, the city of Mamoudzou, which I used as my base for most of my fortnight, is a garbage tip: strays standing up to their bellies in plastic bags, a sieve of potholes for windy tarred roads and all such typically Third World disgraces. Mamoudzou does brag a bank or two, but has yet to handle a Thomas Cook travellers' cheque without suspicion and infuriating day long delays. So travel there with cash to hand and lots of it, for Mayotte is a spectacularly expensive place. The reason is that next to every consumable must be imported.

Yet in Mamoudzou I found my evening strolls in the neat and elaborate Botanic Gardens on the headland of Pointe Mahabou a rare delight. There suitably trendy citizens jog, or picnic, or court, or just chill off together, clacking down dominoes in the scenic belvederes. There Sultan Adriantsouli, the one who sold out his own Malgaches to the House of Bourbon, lies buried in state, saluted by skyhigh coconuts and mangoes and jackfruits and litchis and frangipani and croton and coral hybiscus and poinsettias. At points the cliffs themselves seem held back by giant agaves.

Beneath you extend those submarine prairies where the turtles manoeuvre. You may actually pick them out, like collapsed diningroom tables, grazing the seafloor, coming up for air. Opposite is one of many islets, this one being a reserve for the kind of lemur the sultan brought with him from Madagascar as a pet. Called makis, these long-tailed, furry, orange-eyed bundles are everywhere in the canopies, avoiding the ground for fear of dogs. Sit on a public bench, making the most of peeling a banana, and a maki will vault on to your shoulder, snort into your ear and then steal the fruit from your fist. So will a tumble of six others. Then they swing off, fly between branches, arms outstretched.

So do those fruitbats. The first I spotted I thought must be some raptor blown in from the continent. But on Mayotte you have to become accustomed to the notion that bats may cruise like that and by daylight, too. Unlike the French surveillance patrols, the giant bats of Mayotte are not equipped with radar and so cannot harvest by night. They are a spiky, chittering lot; they even squabble in mid-air. Then they hook themselves out to dry upside down, like old laundry, in any bare tree. They are also protected, as a tourist attraction. And so are the triton shells, because they eat up the starfish, which threaten to eat up the coral belt.

All of Mayotte has well mapped hiking routes. I found I could walk the island just as readily as hire a taxi with a guide to cover the limited infrastructure of roads. Friendliness is their way, each and everyone on the tracks managing at least a polite "Bonjour". There is one rule, however; speak French in reply, for English is practically unheard of there. The second rule is: speak more French.

Mayotte has limited schooling available, with little of it in English. For further education, the Mahorais youth has to be transferred to Réunion, or indeed to France itself. There, especially in the port of Marseilles, all old seafarers from Mayotte have collected, forming a colony of their own in support of their next generation.

Apart from the official language of French, so diverse is the island's linguistic heritage that there are neighbouring villages up in the bush that to this day cannot understand one another. In one they speak Sakalava, in the next it's a Swahili derivative, albeit their base language is Arabic, learnt in Koranic school. The very name 'Mayotte' derives from the Arabic word 'maouti'. Maouti rather darkly means death itself, a label bestowed on this smoky paradise because of its hazardous passages to be piloted through, and its medieval reputation for shipwrecking. Sindbad the sailor was cast up here and felt it must be some calamitous monster.

From the steep peak above it, Mamoudzou certainly does look forbidding – an infernally lit human sump under lowering thunderheads. When the clouds burst, the downpour is pitiless, even though May to September – coinciding conveniently with the European peak tourist season – is supposed to be the dry period. In October the real storms begin and, of course, so does the cyclone season. That is why, as in all the region, Mayotte architecture is squat, bunkered down, self-protective. In those mountainside settlements: no more than bamboo and mud, soon flattened, but easily reconstructed.

Owing to the population increase, Mayotte is a place of children. They always seem to have splotchy butterflies hanging about them. More than once I came upon a whole kindergarten tribe, out labouring with machetes, far from any adult supervision. One span were right up at the House of the Governor, a historic site built once upon a time for his lordship to recuperate from the malaria. They were foraging in the jungle, instructed to bring back fodder for the backyard zebu in town. Hence forests of branches scampering along on bare feet. And their parents, they tell me, are still polygamous.

One work-site I came across certainly stopped me in my tracks. This was at Bandrélé, in the shade of towering baobabs, and recently declared an eco-museum. There large mamas were boiling the mud from the tidal swamp underfoot in a complicated process, eventually to crystallise out the pure salt. It was the little girls treading sludge, shovelling it into wheelbarrows, I felt doubtful about, while the daughters of the privileged invaders in their coastal retreats had merely to shake salt out of the cellars of Cerebos. Cerebos is imported, too, like Castél (which we would call Castle Lager) and Coke and dozens of other ordinary comestibles. For the blistered, bleeding, salt-treading waif it's just more manioc she had to look forward to, with a slice of tomato. For her grandmother, making charcoal, a paper-screw of peanuts.

One unique feature of the settlements away from the developed tourist spots is the 'banga'. They have nothing to do with marijuana, which is merely another of the island's incessant fragrances. A banga is what the village's swains, once their moustaches start to sprout, are expected to group together and put up away from their swarming families. They have to build them for themselves (out of palm-fronds and Hewlett Packard thrown out packing mostly) as study dorms, and in them they practise how to read and write. They paint messages to their future beloveds on the walls outside: BIG SEXY AIME AÏCHA, in bright red, was my favourite. Best of all, bangas are decorated fantastically and thus may enter cross-island competitions.

All this is pass-the-time activity, while their elders are out in their pirogues in that immensity of the dazzling Indian Ocean. On hand-lines they haul up tuna, bonito, speckled parrot-fish ... And still the main social event in Mamoudzou is the boats coming in to market. There the catch is examined and divided and subdivided, and then sliced. A whole octopus may go for 25 centimes, which is less than R2.00.

The offshore fringe of Mayotte is said to contain the most biologically diverse wonderland, available to the skilled diver, well catered for by the Nautical Clubs which have access to the littoral. For the non-diver life on land remains undeveloped: I counted only four swimming-pools in the entire territory. By contrast, overnighting to change planes on Réunion, I noticed an autoroute blocked because a crane had dropped one of a thousand prefab, one-piece pools in the middle of it.

Rather, on backwater Mayotte, I found myself ambling along under a vast hat, stopping at every stall and wooden bistro, with the locals joining my sweaty promenade, just to chat a bit and for lack of anything better to do. I suggested they could perhaps form up for soccer. On Mayotte only women play soccer!

One day, those lounging lads hoped, a select few of them would reach the metropole. Meanwhile, for example, there was always basket-braiding to occupy them, staged as a race! And hustling the hatched baby turtles down to the shallows before any predators could get them! And the blast and brush of a whale's tail! So then, souvenirs of the millennium of the slavery system that had landed them there were all gone? Yes, it was Afro-Reggae today. And as for the old gin-soaked planters with their grinding refineries? They were rusty ruins now.

When I had to leave Mayotte, with its runny hillsides and combers licking through coves and misty bayous and kreef and tamarind juice and the music of the souk, and mosquito coils and dripping air-conditioners on the veranda overlooking never-ending shoals ... I had a send-off delegation accompanying me. From the very basic but hospitable Oasis Hotel, to the marketplace, the famous ferry, the crammed taxi and to the airport where that Boeing came in. They accompanied me there with my bulging suitcase. It was full of printed cloths and aromatic soaps and essences and a bit of the coconut an aerialist had hacked off and lobbed down to me. And the same good tourism officials who had welcomed me solemnly shook hands again to say farewell. And we all shared a last Liquifruit and my packet of Baumann's biscuits.

Then they all stood against the fence while the aircraft closed up. As it wheeled around and took off, they would be clapping.

Two Weeks in Tana

I arrived on one of three direct Sunday flights from Johannesburg, eastwards across the Indian Ocean into Antananarivo. I was just in time to catch the end of South Africa Week, held to mark our Freedom Day, with a competitive walk through the narrow cobbled streets, across canals, down paths all bearing the rutted scars of the recent rainy season. So South Africans were beginning at last to invade Madagascar, our island neighbour half our size and only three and a bit hours away.

Soon enough I learnt a key phrase there was 'Durban 2003', meaning the World Parks Congress at which participants pledged not only to fight poverty, but to do so by persuading communities to follow the new buzzwords: promote 'eco-tourism' and preserve 'biodiversity'. Thus our export to them was a now chic 'green revolution'.

This was signified by the local Wildlife Conservation Society mounting sophisticated 4 x 4 expeditions, with extra spare tyres, to somewhere out there in their wrinkled, smoky, rusty hinterland, where only the rice paddies are flat. As everyone must know by now, in Madagascar there are 51 species of lemur which leap about the remaining indigenous forests; there are dozens of types of flagrant chameleons, sticking out their tongues at the rarest orchids; the birds are all quite different; and sumptuous butterflies expose themselves, then clap together and disappear. That is, not to mention bossed whales cavorting and trees that are anthropophagous.

Such is the endemic life of the world's lost sixth continent. The nearest I got to any spectacular spotting and twitching, though, I confess, was an endangered geometric giant tortoise in someone's garden. It kept trying to ram my ankle.

But the genial capital has more than enough sights to entertain the raw visitor, especially its famous markets. Once in the Sixties Nadine Gordimer wrote in a travel piece of stepping down into the valley from her hotel to the famous Zoma, or Friday market, and she felt it was like making an entrance. Slow to take the hint, I was dropped off forty years later at the bookstall end, with everything removable of mine zipped in or strapped on. I made the classic mistake of announcing my interest first thing – Malagasy poetry, written in French – only to be pursued by 160 stallholders with faded copies of the 1960 edition of the works of the great Jean-Joseph Rabéarivelo, founding father of their culture. After a long zigzag chase, I settled with the crowd – for one copy only, and at a quarter the initial price. Later at the Lutheran Bible bookshop I actually picked up an item called *Les Fleurs de L'Îsle Rouge*, dated 1947 and still in print. Other than those, it's faded late Lenin on display, dating from the country's dire regime of the Eighties, alongside *Le Petit Prince* and second-hand copies of *Paris-Match*, all freckling in the drizzle.

I was to spend my fortnight exploring Antananarivo, or Tananarive as the French who occupied it from 1896 to 1960 rendered it, or just plain Tana. From the colonial railway station (disused) runs the central Avenue of Independence, where the French expatriates gather, double parking on the pavements, slapping down their keys and the rare cellphone on café tables. Each is twice the size of any locals. Their toddlers carry baguettes longer than themselves. On the terrace all are forbidden by law to exchange currencies. Nor for that matter may one deal in rare stones (rubies and sapphires), mined in the potholes down where the country straddles athwart the Tropic of Capricorn.

One such establishment features an ice-cream parlour, where all except one of the flavours are imported directly from Paris. The exception is the Red Island's tangy, dangling vanilla. At the Hilton's Bistro, speciality of the day usually is 'Poêle de Crocodile à la Provençale' (i.e. fried croc). Served with, not polished or brown or long-grained rice, but with red rice.

Soon I discovered the half-price Snack-Resto in the Tahala Raharihasina, which is the artists' warren. In the kitchen there is a warm-up on valiha (the sweet-sounding erect tube strung with wire) and tamtams (drums). Alongside is an aerobics session, considered to be highly 'underground', for barefoot young maidens.

Here I had my introduction to fruits I had never heard of, like the kaki (a sort of sweet tomato) and the huge pomme cannelle or cinnamon apple. Then there is the corossol or custard apple, the white juice of which one would like to swim in. Here I also had a thoughtful conversation with an old-fashioned bootblack. Apparently Kiwi Polish, much advertised and Made in France, is out. It has to be Lube. So I had my walking boots Lubed while I sucked the ice of my juice.

Above the Snack-Resto gather the Malgache writers and their protégés, elaborating the Malagasy language which has united all the diverse groups of the island for at least a millennium and which I learn is Malayo-Indonesian in origin. With their adapters from French and increasingly English, the intention is to update their heritage to meet globalised technical standards. That is the task of the Union des Poètes et Écrivains de Madagascar, over half a century old, and now actually called Havatsa. Havatsa means to mark life with a stamp.

Other indigenous words I had to acquire in a hurry. One travel agent I queried threw her hands up when I suggested I might escape Tana on a two-day trip down to the port of Tamatave (or rather Toamasina), on the east side. It was riddled with 'paludisme', she warned me, which I knew was malaria, against which I was routinely on prophylaxis anyway. But there was also the 'dengue' fever, which I thought I could also handle. But alarmingly there was also now the terrible-sounding 'chikungunya', a painful and never-ending kind of joint-creaking, inter-island epidemic of sleeping sickness. When I remarked that, at my advanced age, I thought I probably had that anyway, she was not amused. So Tamatave was strictly out of bounds, as was everywhere else you would not risk reaching in a private car.

One look at the potholes full of tadpoles, the mosquitoes circulating like wire mobiles, and I was indeed discouraged. Rather take a prepaid, organised group tour than venture out in a crowded taxi-brousse, or bush-taxi, or even in a decrepit, rickety pousse-pousse. Which is a museum piece of a ricksha. (So many words the French infantilised by repeating them, like pilipili for piri-piri. But try this for the Cape gooseberry: pokpok.)

As for Tana by night, that was out of reach too. I quote from the official government warning to all obvious-looking tourists: "Walking after hours is not safe, including in the areas around Western-standard hotels. Organised groups of bandits patrol areas where foreigners congregate."

So I was gated to my safe, friendly guest house up the slopes, the evening escape from downtown being a hair-raising taxi-ride – through the rush-hour byways crammed with all the various populations, plus weary shoulder-humped zebus, scraggy chickens, waste-removal trucks, carts piled high and pulled uphill by human traction. The taxi-driver who insisted on adopting me may be described as follows: splay-toed bare brown feet, steering with spanner in his fist. In a jam he would switch off and dash out to decant a cupful of fuel into the tank from his thermos. Switch off again for the slopes. No lights. When we discussed and agreed on his fee each time (5 000 ariary), he would still figure it in the previous Malagasy francs at five times as much. Total cost: R16.

My daytime base in the city centre was at the Centre Culturel Albert Camus, which thanks to the French government provides the country's main library facilities and animates its entertainment calendar. From there I could hike about with a map that indicated none of the original twelve sacred hills over which Antananarivo was planned, let alone the six more over which with its population of over one million it has spread, nor any of the eroded crevasses into which it threatens to collapse.

At the summit of this High Plateau is the Palace of the Queens who ruled from on top throughout the nineteenth century. Alas, it was gutted by fire ten years ago and is still under reconstruction. On hand for Her Majesty was her prime minister, whose own spectacular three-storey palace is open to visitors with its historic collection. For the rest the island's history is situated in competitive churches, the Protestant cathedral on the cliffside here, the Catholic one there. They are very impressive on the woody skyline where 'Jesoa Kristy' rules.

Ambling through the older picturesque houses is constantly arresting. Usually they are three storeyed as well, with views from rusty, tiled, steeply-sloping attic mansards over the wide plains below. Most Victorian looking mansions are made of reddish brick, with colourful shutters and wooden balconies, often with the stairs outside. Alongside crowded convents and Shoprite outlets they seem incongruous relics, yet all disparities are reconciled by a dazzling, straggling overgrowth of giant poinsettias, frangipani, cascades of golden shower and cassia. Alongside these upright villas, which persist even in the furthest countryside behind laterite walls, to break up their severity are floppy bananas and inevitably the emblem of Air Madagascar, the fan-shaped traveller's palm.

To track down the record of some long forgotten, early South African links with Madagascar, I was admitted to their National Library. Several London Missionary Society eminences moved to Tana after a stint at the Cape of Good Hope, the Rev. William Ellis being one. He brought with him a camera and all the collodion apparatus. In 1858 he produced the first ever travel book to be illustrated with photographs, and in Antananarivo the LMS printing works is still running.

After the Second Anglo-Boer War, the exiled Deneys Reitz attempted to set up a transport business here. In despair he wrote his classic memoir of the fight, *Commando*, dating it Antananarivo, 1903.

In the library, packed with young scholars, the catalogue cards still curl about their rods in wooden cabinets; no computers in this establishment and there is moss growing on the ferns. As for a photocopying service ... I had to be escorted with an armful of the reviews in which Madagascans wrote of their unique war exploits on Boer terrain to the Indian shop a few streets away. There a huge portrait of Mother Teresa blessed the collapsing xerox machine, encouraging it to work.

Nearby is one of the city's many placid lakes, called Anosi. A causeway thrusts across to the island in the middle, where a monument commemorates those fallen in fighting to defend the colonial motherland abroad. Less remembered is that it was a largely South African-led invasion which delivered this country from its Nazi rulers of Vichy in 1942. A vast heronry chatters on undisturbed. Over the water one hears the clacking rattle made by peanut sellers and the calling for customers of the barbers in decorated stalls. Then a howling crowd, fists raised, charges through the lanes of traffic – they are after a pickpocket.

Thus I grew incredibly fond of spitting, pissing, shitting Antananarivo, with its white, green and red flag everywhere; its modest 'hotelys' advertising the inevitable THB (Three Horses Beer – delicious); the touts hawking tripods and high-chairs and Raybans and belts and La Vache qui Rit and the six daily (excellent) newspapers and even Bonbon Anglais (which is a lemonade), leaving aside the actual heads of zebus mounted with their polished, semicircular horns. Many of the traditional handicrafts have gone, naturally. In the Archeological Museum was the old national dress of the lamba, woven exquisitely of cotton or even of silk in sumptuous patterns, to adorn the most striking men and women of old. And raffia shopping baskets, dyed a devastating purple. And decorated umbrellas.

But nowadays 'Nobody likes the poor', as my landlady remarked, and of course Madagascar is famous now for its record-breaking poverty. In one of the tunnels under the hills I was horrified to stumble across a beggar woman on the narrow pavement, her ragged children comatose with traffic emissions. Apart from the herons, Tana is birdless – apart from urchins, that is, who imitate birdcalls in knobbly passageways with whistles. All that flies is their kites made of plastic bags, rising in the sunlight against stormclouds, out of the sprawling slums. Nobody likes the poor indeed, without electricity and refrigeration, fresh water and so on. All they have is barking mongrels and a banknote or two curled about like a bat's ear, or like a tobacco leaf which might just as well be smoked. Hardly a euro for the duty free. They don't even wear braids.

A final image of my visit. Antananarivo has no mowers, either. So we have a dusky lad with a garbage bag clipping the overgrown lawn of the administrative centre, the Avenue of Independence, with a pair of shears. He is to steal away the falling clumps, to fuel the beast of burden of his boss, down some rotting canal. He is a clandestine who has escaped by boat from the Comoros and has no papers. He is humming a rice-gathering song, interspersed with a gobbling sound – a turkey-cock. In his veins run the bloods of Asia, Persia, Africa and of Europe. He tells me he does own a concertina, though, which will assist him in his courtship.

Time to turn one's back. He stops me by saying he would like to visit South Africa, some day.

ACKNOWLEDGEMENTS

The publishers are grateful to the following copyright-holders for permission to reproduce the following original works:

in France, *Présence Africaine* for Assane Diallo's poem and for Jacques Rabémananjara's two poems; *Revue Noire* for Henry Koombes's poem; L'Harmattan for two poems by Mahamoud M'Saidie and two items by Abdou S. Baco; La Pensée Universelle for two poems by Jean-Georges Prosper; Pierre Jean Oswald for four poems from *Contes et Poèmes des Seychelles* by Antoine Abel; Via Valeriano for an excerpt from Salim Hatubou's *Metro Bougainville*; and Thierry Sajat for four poems by Kamaroudine Abdallah Paune;

on Réunion, Azalées Editions for three poems by Khal; to Boris Gamaleya for his poem and also to Claire Karm for hers; to Collection la Roche Écrite, Éditions Grand Ocean, for the poem by Esther Nirina and the two poems by Vololona Picard;

on Mauritius, the estates of Malcolm de Chazal and of Pierre Renaud for their items; to Ng Kwet Chan for three poems, to Carl de Souza for his item and to Sedley Assonne for his poem, as well as to Édouard J. Maunick, resident in South Africa, for his three poems;

in Madagascar, to the following: Flavien Ranaivo, the estate of Dox, Elie-Charles Abraham, Thomas Rahandraha, Henri Rahaingoson, Serge Henri Rodin, Élie Rajaonarison, David Jaomanoro and Jean-Luc Raharimanana; also to Veromanitra Razafiarivony, Ndrivo Andriamboavonjy, Tombo Ravalihasy and Lazawell Adriamiariseta, as well as Adjmaël Halidi for his five items;

on the Comoros, to KomÉdit publishers of Moroni for two poems by Aboubacar Saïd Salim, the five items by Saïndoune Ben Ali and the excerpt by Nassuf Djailani;

on Mayotte, to Amir Mounib and Moussa Abdou each for their single contributions, as well as to Les Éditions du Baobab of La Maison des Livres for the three poems by Yazidou Maandhui.

See also the section "Notes on Translators" for further acknowledgements, with thanks for translated works as listed.

In some cases, despite every effort, the publishers have not been able to be in touch with copyright-holders of original items or of their translations. The publishers would be grateful if any such parties would contact them at Protea Book House, P.O. Box 35110, Menlo Park, 0102, South Africa, so that appropriate corrections may be made in any subsequent printing.

The publishers are also grateful to the French Institute of South Africa (IFAS), the Embassy of France in South Africa and Alliance Française of Johannesburg for their generous contribution and assistance, specifically Mr. Frédéric Jagu of these institutions for facilitating communication between the publishers and authors.

INDEX

Abdou, Moussa, 178
Abel, Antoine, xxxi, 144
Abraham, Elie-Charles, 109
Ali, Saïndoune Ben, 157
Allain, Robert-Jules, 96
Andriamiariseta, Lazawell, 139
Andrianarahinjaka, Lucien, 113
Armstrong, James C., xxxi
Assonne, Sedley Richard, 78
Attoumani, Nassur, xx
Baco, Abdou S., xx, 157, 175
Battiss, Walter, xix
Baudelaire, Charles, xxxvii, 6, 196–200
Beckett, Carole, xxi, xxxiv, xxxviii, 151, 172
Beier, Ulli, xxv
Belair, Alain, 44, 192
Bernardin de Saint-Pierre, Jacques-Henri, xxviii, 1, 12, 54, 196
Bertin, Antoine de, 41
Blair, Dorothy S., xxxvii, 84, 88, 113
Bourgeacq, Jacques, 102, 133
Brézé, Jean, xxii,
Bulpin, T.V., xviii
Cabon, Marcel, 56
Camo, Pierre, 83
Camoens, Luis de, 209
Campbell, Roy, xxxvii, 6, 8–9
Camus, Albert, xxvi
Cazamian, André, 41
Cesaire, Aimé, xxiii
Chan, Clifford Ng Kwet, 64
Changkye, Eddy J., 51
Chasle, Raymond, xxxv
Chazal, Malcolm de, xxxii, 54

Chevrier, Jacques, xxv
Collen, Lindsey, xxii
Collet, Joseph, xxxv
Craveirinha, José, 203
Cubitt, Gerald, xix
Davenant, William, xvi
Davis, Edward, xxxvii, 7
Dayot, Eugène, 21
Defoe, Daniel, xv, 211
Devi, Ananda, xxii
Diallo, Assane Y., 13
Djailani, Nassuf, xx–xxi, 180
Dox, 106
Dumas, Alexandre, 4
Elbadawi, Soeuf, 157
Ellis, William, 226
Fabre, Michel, xxxi
Falla, Jonathan, xiii
Fanon, Frantz, xxi
Faure-Vidot, Maggie, xxxi
Feuser, Willfried, 113
Finn, Julio, xxvii
Fox, Leonard, xxi–xxii
Gage, Jennifer, xxxv
Gamaleya, Boris, 42
Gascoyne, David, xxxiv
Gauvin, Axel, xxii
Georges-François, Pierre-Claude, 35
Gordimer, Nadine, 222
Grare, Christabel, 44, 56
Halidi, Adjmaël, 157, 168
Haring, Lee, xxi
Hart, Robert-Edward, xxxii, 51, 96
Hart de Keating, Stefan, xxxv
Hatubou, Salim, 161

231

Hughes, Langston, xxiv
Jacques, François, 101
Jaomanoro, David, 126
Joubert, Elsa, xix
Joubert, Jean-Louis, xxiii
Karm, Claire, 48
Kassam, Amin, xiii
Kazantzakis, Nikos, 211
Keineg, Paol, xxxiv
Kelly, Michael, xxvii
Kennedy, Ellen Conroy, xxvi, 60
Kesteloot, Lilyan, xxv, 102
Kgositsile, Keorapetse, 60
Khal, xxvii, 76
Knopfli, Rui, xiv
Koombes, Henry, 71
Koshland, Miriam, xxiv, xxxvii–xxviii, 84, 87, 101, 103
Leconte de Lisle, Charles René Marie, 6, 25, 151, 192
Leeb-du Toit, Lucienne, 56
Leipoldt, C. Louis, 199
L'Homme, Léoville, xxxii
Maandhui, Yazidou, xx, 182
Malim, Michael, xviii, 51
Mancham, James, xxix, 206
Mannoni, Octave, 101
Maponya, Maishe, 98
Marimoutou, Carpanin, xxii
Masson, Loys, xxxiv
Maunick, Édouard J., xxv, xxvii, xxxi–xxxii, 51, 60–61, 111, 113
Maury, Pierre, xxxiii
Moore, Gerald, xxv
Mounib, Amir, xx, 167
M'Saidie, Mahamoud, 155
Mugot, Hazel, xxix
Murphy, Richard, xiv
Ndrivo, 135

Neethling, Joan, xxxviii, 11, 40, 47
Nirina, Esther, 111
Okala, Lennard, xiv
Okri, Ben, 159
Ommanney, F. D., xviii, xxxi–xxxii, 143
Ozoux, Louis, 39, 192
Parny, Évariste, 17, 41, 129, 197
Paulhan, Jean, 102
Paune, Kamaroudine Abdallah, 162
Picard, Vololona, 129
Preller, Alexis, xix
Prosper, Jean-Georges, 64, 68, 76
Rabéarivelo, Jean-Joseph, xxi–xxvii, xxxiii, xxxvii, 42, 83–84, 96–98, 101, 116, 133, 223
Rabémananjara, Jacques, xxiii–xxv, xxvii, xxxv, 13, 97–98, 113, 122
Radiguet, Raymond, 12
Rahaingoson, Henri, xxxiii, 116
Rahandraha, Thomas, 97, 113
Raharimanana, Jean-Luc, xxiii, 98, 133
Rajaonarison, Élie, xxxiii, 122
Rajemisa-Raolison, Régis, 109
Rakotoson, Michèle, xxiii
Ramarosoa, Liliane, xxiii, 113, 133
Ranaivo, Flavien, xxiii, xxvi, xxxiv, 101–102, 122
Rauville, Camille de, 54
Ravalihasy, Tombo, 137
Razafiarivony, Veromanitra, 131
Reed, John, xxv–xxvi
Reitz, Deneys, 226
Renaud, Pierre, 56, 64
Reygnault, Christiane, xxiv
Rodin, Serge Henri, xxxiii, 121, 168
Rutherfoord, Peggy, xxxvii
Salim, Aboubacar Saïd, 151

Samlong, Jean-François, xxii
Sartre, Jean-Paul, xxiii, 159
Senghor, Léopold Sédar, xxiii–xxv,
    13, 54, 84
Sepamla, Sipho, 98
Silva, Hazel de, xxix
Sousa, Carl de, 73
Slater, Candace, xxxiv
Soyinka, Wole, xxvii
Stern, Irma, xix
Stockenström, Wilma, xxxviii, 10,
    102, 104
Strike, Norman, 61
Taylor, John, 42
Tlali, Miriam, 98
Toihiri, Mohamed, xx
Victor, Patrick, xxxii
Wake, Clive, xxv–xxvi
Wangeci, Agatha, xiii
Weiss, Irving, 54
Wells, H.G., xvii